Union Voices

Union Voices

*Tactics and Tensions
in UK Organizing*

Melanie Simms, Jane Holgate,
and Edmund Heery

ILR Press
an imprint of
Cornell University Press
Ithaca and London

First published 2013 by Cornell University Press
First printing, Cornell Paperbacks, 2013
Printed in the United States of America and the United Kingdom

Library of Congress Cataloging-in-Publication Data

Simms, Melanie.
    Union voices : tactics and tensions in UK organizing / Melanie Simms,
Jane Holgate, and Edmund Heery.
        p. cm.
    Includes bibliographical references and index.
    ISBN 978-0-8014-5120-1 (cloth : alk. paper)
    ISBN 978-0-8014-7813-0 (pbk. : alk. paper)
    1. Labor unions—Organizing—Great Britain.   2. TUC Organising
Academy.   I. Holgate, Jane.   II. Heery, Edmund.   III. Title.
    HD6490.O72G77   2013
    331.880941—dc23   2012016500

Cornell University Press strives to use environmentally responsible
suppliers and materials to the fullest extent possible in the publishing of
its books. Such materials include vegetable-based, low-VOC inks and
acid-free papers that are recycled, totally chlorine-free, or partly composed
of nonwood fibers. For further information, visit our website at www.
cornellpress.cornell.edu.

Cloth printing   10   9   8   7   6   5   4   3   2   1
Paperback printing   10   9   8   7   6   5   4   3   2   1

CONTENTS

Acknowledgments

Many people have contributed to the writing of this book, although we alone are responsible for any errors. We want particularly to thank the various institutions that have funded parts of the research since 1996, specifically the Nuffield Foundation, Cardiff University, and the Economic and Social Research Council. The Trades Union Congress (TUC) has given us support, access, and sponsorship in kind, and we are very grateful for their help. Our own universities have been extremely supportive, as have those of other institutions we have worked at over the past decade and a half. To our colleagues, we offer thanks for their consistent support in the lengthy process of researching and writing this book. We also thank our colleagues at the Industrial Relations Research Unit at the University of Warwick and the Working Lives Research Institute at London Metropolitan University for their support of and enthusiasm for this project.

Individual unions have also been extremely supportive and patient by allowing us access to campaigns and being generous with their time. We cannot possibly list all of the people who have helped us but they know who they are and we are very grateful. And to the officers, organizers, members, and workers involved in fighting the campaigns we have studied, we offer our profound thanks and best wishes.

Of course, books don't get written without support from those in our lives outside work. To them we also offer our thanks for their continued support, patience, and enthusiasm. La Muse writers' retreat in France also helped make the process possible.

Interested readers can find detailed discussions of the research methods we have used for different phases of the data collection throughout this thirteen-year research project in much of our previous work (see, for example, Simms and Holgate 2010a, 2010b; Simms 2007a, 2007b; Holgate 2005; Heery et al. 2000a, 2000b, 2000c). Nonetheless, it is important to highlight the main bodies of evidence on which we base the comments and discussions that we outline in this book. Between us, we have been studying organizing policy and practice in UK unions since 1996, but we were involved before then as union activists. Initially the research was undertaken by Edmund Heery who became interested in the restructuring of the TUC and its efforts to promote union renewal (Heery 1998a). He carried out a series of around thirty-five interviews between 1996 and 1998, during the time that the TUC was developing the Organising Academy. In 1998, he secured research funding for an initial period of three years, for a project that would involve a researcher being sent to the first year of the Organising Academy training as a participant observer. Melanie Simms was hired as that researcher, and in addition to extensive periods of observation at both training sessions and in the work of organizers during the campaigns they ran, we carried out over the next three years a further set of 120 formal interviews with policymakers, organizers, their coaches and mentors, activists, and other key participants. Some of these were done on the telephone, but most were lengthy face-to-face discussions. And, of course, the periods of observation—and sometimes participation—afforded the opportunity to engage in extensive informal interviewing.

Between 1998 and 2002, we also undertook four important surveys. We surveyed all UK unions on their organizing policy and practice in both 1998 and 2000—before and after the statutory recognition legislation. Between 1998 and 2003, we surveyed all academy organizers during their final training session, asking them for their immediate reflections on their training year. And we also asked them to complete a survey relating to the organizing practices they used in specific organizing campaigns they had been working on. Many of the questions that we used in these surveys replicate each other, which allows a good view of organizing practice at different levels of the unions.

Alongside this, Melanie also started her doctoral research. Following five successful organizing campaigns in detail and over a longitudinal period (1998–2005), she was able to get the kind of in-depth data that were needed to comment on organizing practice in specific contexts. At the same time, for her own doctoral studies, Jane Holgate was undertaking a similarly in-depth study of the particular challenges facing black and ethnic minority workers during organizing campaigns. These "thick descriptions" of UK organizing campaigns have been invaluable to our ability to conceptualize how and why unions, their organizers, and their activists behave in the ways that they do. For this research, between us, we carried out more than two hundred additional interviews and spent large periods of time in these workplaces observing and asking questions.

Last, but not least, in 2006 Jane Holgate and Melanie Simms secured funding from the Nuffield Foundation to go back to the TUC, sponsoring unions, and academy graduates to ask them about their views on what impact the Organising Academy had had over the previous decade. It was always our intention to use the tenth anniversary of the Organising Academy to evaluate the impact of the development of organizing in the United Kingdom. We therefore surveyed all academy graduates about their experiences of their training in retrospect and asked them about where their careers had subsequently taken them. We selected twenty-eight graduates to interview in more depth and asked them about their experiences and views using a biographical narrative interview method (Chamberlayne et al. 2000). Although the biographical narrative method is not common in the field of industrial relations, it is our belief that—even in a modified form as used here—it was particularly useful in our interviews with organizers who were being encouraged to place themselves at the center of the debates around union organizing. The analysis of biographical data is, of course, person centered, but the intention was to draw links between the individual agency of organizers and the wider frameworks in which they were operating and the implication this has for their personal and professional practice where organizing was actually taking place.

We also returned to interview twenty-one key respondents who had been particularly influential in development and training at the academy. In this phase of the research, we carried out short periods (a few days) of observation at each of the specialist training programs set up by three of the largest unions in the United Kingdom: the GMB; the Union of Shop, Distributive, and Allied Workers (USDAW); and Unite. These spin-off academies were an explicit effort by these unions to adapt organizing ideas to their specific contexts, so they were useful to show us what organizing "means" in different sectors and unions. Throughout all of these phases of research we have also collected masses of documentary data. Papers for meetings, flyers, policy documents, collective bargaining agreements, and strategy papers have been among the most useful, but there are plenty of others.

Throughout this time we have developed close links with organizers and other people within the UK union movement. We are eternally grateful for their time, patience, and fortitude; without them, the work could never have happened. We make every effort we can to involve them in our work. In this sense, we are very deeply embedded in the world of union organizing; but our mistakes are purely our own and any criticisms are offered in the spirit of solidarity.

Over the years, we have also presented some aspects of the research at academic conferences and at meetings with trade unionists. Almost all of that material was written by the main authors, but many times the involvement of other members of the extended research team has been extremely valuable. Parts of the discussion about the lives of organizers were presented in a paper written mainly by Rick Delbridge in 2000. We are grateful for his permission to draw on the ideas presented there. Andy Charlwood has undoubtedly influenced our views about how unions engage with their wider environment, and we draw on some of the discussion presented in Simms and Charlwood (2010) in the section about the background to organizing. We have also benefited from extensive discussions with other academics and with trade unionists. We cannot possibly mention them all here, but we fully acknowledge their influence.

UNION VOICES

INTRODUCTION

This book tells the story of what is, in our view, probably the most significant development in British trade unionism of recent years: the increasing focus on organizing activity. We do this by reflecting on the impact of the UK's Trades Union Congress (TUC) Organising Academy (OA), the participants in the training program, and the organizing campaigns that union organizers have run. We explicitly want to give voice to these union activists who have worked so hard to recruit and organize new union members. Much has already been written in the United Kingdom (often by us) about these developments but what is often lost in short articles or surveys are the stories that organizers have to tell. In an effort to build a base of knowledge from which to start to analyze changes, we have so far tended to focus on publishing the studies that demonstrate general trends and developments. This book seeks to do something slightly different. We draw on those previously published papers where necessary, but here we want to engage with the politics and tensions behind those trends; both on a macro and a micro level. We want to tell the stories of what organizing is "like" on the front line, what organizers do, and how they do it. The workplace struggles of workers and their unions are at the heart of these stories. But we also want to draw attention to the wider reasons why union organizing is important. As we will argue, one of the things that happened as ideas about organizing migrated from other countries—notably the United States and Australia—to the United Kingdom is that the political conceptualization of why unions are organizing has been underexamined. We want to understand and examine organizing as a political process, and we want to look at the politics within the union but also the wider purpose of organizing, which often varies from context to context.

In 1998, the TUC took the bold step of opening the doors of a training academy for union organizers. This move was bold for a number of reasons. First, historically the TUC has been mainly a coordinating organization for UK unions rather than a body that leads particular initiatives. The Organising Academy was explicitly informed by a desire to promote a particular form of trade unionism that encouraged member participation and activism. This was a significant departure from the usual role of the TUC, which has been mainly to establish consensus-based policy that takes account of the interests of a very broad range of affiliate unions (Heery 1998a). But it was a bold step for one other crucial reason that is rarely discussed: it was an explicit attempt to "shake up" the trade union movement by recruiting new people to work in the unions. Although Organising Academy participants all had some experience in campaigning and activism, it was not always gained in the labor movement. The establishment of the academy offered an opportunity to work in the union movement, bypassing the conventional career structure of serving many years as a union representative before becoming an officer for an individual union. In the early years, organizers were frequently referred to as the "next leaders of the union movement" despite the potential that this could create a dangerous hostage to fortune. There was recognition from the highest levels of the TUC and participating unions that the organizers they sought to recruit and train would be very different from existing union officers and leaders. In general, it was hoped that they would be younger, with a more diverse range of experiences prior to working in unions, and crucially, that they would be more representative of the workforce in respect of gender and ethnicity.

So why did the TUC feel sufficiently emboldened to take on this role? The figures on union decline throughout the 1980s and 1990s have been well documented: declining membership, declining income, declining bargaining coverage, failure to organize new sectors and workplaces, and a decline in union power (see Simms and Charlwood 2010 for a fuller overview) all contributed to a context within which the TUC saw a clear role to intervene in renewal efforts. Further, British trade unionism has a long-established history of workplace activism, and the structures of many unions rely on workplace membership to campaign and improve working conditions. Indeed, during the periods of union strength this was often considered to be a problematic feature of British trade unionism (Donovan Commission 1968). But attacks on trade unionism by the state during the neoliberal Conservative Party era from 1979 to 1997 meant that many unions were forced by declining membership rolls, income, and activism to focus on managing decline. That is not to say that unions did nothing during that period. Many still actively campaigned on behalf of the Labour Party, and they campaigned against public-sector cuts and other policies that were problematic for their members. They were engaged with notable campaigns against racism such as the lengthy fight for justice for Stephen Lawrence—a young black man murdered in London in 1993—and they consistently continued to develop relationships with employers that would provide the basis for bargaining and improvement of working conditions. The central problem, however, was that social, economic, and political changes made it very difficult to achieve any substantial renewal. Efforts to establish largely cooperative and consensual "partnerships" with employers came under sustained attack in many workplaces with workers reluctant to join ineffective unions and managers reluctant to pay attention to such unions (Jenkins 2007). The notion of working in partnership also came in for political and academic criticism (Kelly 1996) and has become very much less important in the story of British trade unionism than it was ten years ago (Heery et al. 2003c), although it remains an important approach in the public sector (Bacon and Samuel 2009).

Nonetheless, the TUC has been keen to promote both organizing activity and partnership, sometimes side by side. Although this seemed paradoxical to many commentators at the time (Carter and Fairbrother 1998), it reflected a degree of pragmatism within the TUC to try every possible avenue that might encourage union growth (Heery 2002). As part of this effort to promote an internal revitalization as well as a broader effort of union renewal, the TUC launched a comprehensive review of its structures and policies in 1994 (Heery 2002), eventually leading to the establishment of the TUC's New Unionism project, which had the objective of promoting organizing activity. Senior trade unionists traveled to the United States and Australia several times throughout the mid-1990s, explicitly seeking to learn from innovative initiatives such as the AFL-CIO's Organizing Institute and ACTU's Organising Works program in Australia. These programs strongly influenced the thinking of senior UK policymakers within the TUC and affiliate unions.

By 1996 it was clear that, excepting extraordinary circumstances, it was likely that the Labour Party would win the 1997 general election, signaling the end of eighteen years of right-wing Conservative Party dominance of UK politics. Although the Labour Party was keen to signal to the voting public that there would be a policy of "fairness, not favors" toward the trade unions, and certainly that there would not be any repeal of the legislation that seriously constrains the ability of UK unions to take industrial action, there was a formal recognition that trade unions still contributed around 40 percent of Labour Party funds, and that workers' rights were a core part of the 1997 Labour manifesto. To this end, a commitment was secured to enact legislation that would allow unions to force employers to recognize them for the purposes of collective bargaining if they had the support of the majority of the workforce. Although the devil is always in the details of such statutory recognition legislation, and there were many critics of the way in which the legislation was developed (Dickens and Hall 2006), the Employment Relations Act of 1999 delivered this manifesto commitment, and was subsequently revised and updated in 2004.

From the mid-1990s onward, it was clear that the UK union movement, and the TUC specifically, was gearing up to operate in a changed political and institutional climate. This was an important rationale of the development of the Organising Academy: unions needed specialist, trained organizers to take advantage of the opportunities afforded by statutory recognition legislation as well as developments such as the establishment of a national minimum wage in 1999, the introduction of new information and consultation rights for workers as a consequence of European Union legislation, and a shift in the general context of employment relation toward one of benign tolerance of union involvement. It was hoped that these political and legal changes would herald a more auspicious era for trade unionism in general. Inspired by developments abroad, the New Unionism task group launched the Organising Academy as a one-year training program for specialist organizers, with its first intake in 1998. The purpose was largely to train these specialists in organizing tactics and ideas so that they could be agents of a wider cultural change within the union movement.

Cultural Change

The objectives of the TUC Academy were always much broader than simply training specialist organizers to take advantage of opportunities to gain new recognition agreements with employers. Informed by the particular approach underpinning ideas of organizing in the United States and Australia, the academy developed an underlying rationale that in order to appeal to workers who had never previously joined a union, the culture of unions would have to change. Emphasis was placed on membership participation and improving the representativeness of the union movement, particularly in relation to age, gender, ethnicity, and sectoral presence. Beyond the objectives of participative democracy and representativeness, there was also a realization that most unions would struggle to achieve those objectives without committing considerable resources. The TUC generally avoided discussing exact targets, but US discussions about aiming to commit 10 percent of union resources to organizing activity were discussed by senior policymakers. None, however, were specific about whether this was an aspirational target or an achievable target. Equally, none were specific about whether this should be measured as 10 percent of income, 10 percent of expenditure, or 10 percent of activity.

Importantly, and in contrast to organizing activity in some countries, there was an explicit realization that organizing should include both expansionist activity into workplaces where employers did not have an established relationship with unions, and "infill" activity were there was an agreement on the union's representation rights, but where membership, activism, and participation were falling short of expectations. One of the key, senior TUC policymakers promoting the launch of the TUC Academy noted that this had always been an issue of tension:

When we first started...we always emphasized the twin-track approach. We said it had to be rebuilding where we had strands but often membership had fallen to 40 percent in workforces. And it had to be breaking into new areas. But interestingly people only ever heard the breaking into the new areas. And that was the bit that was seen as controversial and those who opposed the agenda alighted upon. (Frances O'Grady, TUC deputy general secretary)

So, it is clear that the objectives of the Organising Academy were manifold, and five core objectives can be identified from the debates and rationales that were presented at the time:

- to recruit and train a cadre of specialist organizers which includes attracting new people to work in the union movement;
- to increase membership and participation in new and existing workplaces, including targeting underrepresented workers for union membership and to encourage their activism;
- to encourage unions to invest a greater proportion of their resources in organizing activity;
- to encourage expansionist activity to nonunionized sectors and workplaces;
- to promote a specific approach to trade unionism, which emphasizes membership involvement and participation.

These capture the ambition of the initiative and the breadth of the objectives. But the danger with this introduction so far is that it risks suggesting that organizing did not exist in the United Kingdom prior to the mid-1990s. Clearly this is untrue. The UK labor movement has a long history of effective workplace, sectoral, professional, and national organization, but there are two crucial differences about the developments in the mid-1990s. The first difference is the notion that organizing should be a particular initiative that demands trained, skilled professional specialists; the second is that these specialists should promote wide and deep culture change and renewal within the labor movement. This ambition developed, in part, as a consequence of a small number of charismatic leaders working internationally to promote these ideas. And in part it reflected growing academic evidence from other countries that increasingly supported the argument that organizing "works" (notably the seminal book by Bronfenbrenner et al. 1998). Because of these ambitions and the way in which organizing initiatives developed in the United Kingdom in the mid-1990s, it is important to note the importance of the transfer of the notion of an organizing "model" in relation to the tactics these new recruits were being trained to use. This is a deeply contested idea within UK trade unionism that has generated considerable debate among both academics and practitioners (de Turberville 2004, Simms and Holgate 2010a), so it is important to outline here how and why we think the idea of an organizing "model" is problematic.

The Organizing "Model"?

The term *organizing model* seemed to enter into handbooks and guidance for labor activists in the United States in the mid to late 1980s (Hurd 1998, 23) and became commonplace in the decade afterward. It is possible that it may have been a term used earlier than that, but our interest in the idea emerges from this period. Most authors and practitioners would agree that the term *organizing* is used to describe an approach to union building that relies on unions facilitating local leadership at the workplace level so that workers are empowered to act for themselves (Heery, Simms, Simpson, et al. 2000). Its purpose is to foster self-reliance and collective identity, organizing around issues in the workplace, which can then lead to increased recruitment and sustained organizing. Importantly, the idea of an organizing "model" was explicitly contrasted with a servicing "model" (Blyton and Turnbull 2004). The former was far more concerned with promoting membership activism while the latter was primarily interested in providing an efficient and effective service to justify the cost of union membership.

However, from the very early stages of this nomenclature entering academic and practitioner debate, there was a great deal of discussion about its meaning and relevance. Added to this, the logic of the organizing and servicing analysis emerged in different national contexts and took on different rationales as the ideas were translated into new countries, new unions, and new sectors. The notion of a "model" was given additional credibility and impetus with the publication of several important pieces of work undertaken by Kate Bronfenbrenner, which presented evidence from National Labor Relations Board (NLRB) data in the United States showing that campaigns that used a range of organizing tactics simultaneously were more effective in securing a first contract than those that just used one or two tactics (Bronfenbrenner and Juravich 1998). The lesson seemed clear; organizers needed to use a "bundle" of tactics together rather than just picking out one or two.

Within some conceptualizations of organizing there are also some important political ideas, including but not limited to, social movement unionism (Turner and Hurd 2001), worker self-organization (Markowitz 2000), principles of anarcho-syndicalism (Lerner 1992, Rachleff 1999), and arguments about changing the labor movement (Turner et al. 2001). As these ideas transferred to the United Kingdom, researchers and practitioners tried to better understand what these different aspects of organizing meant in the UK context. An early effort to do this was made by the Cardiff research team. They (we) adopted the terminology of an organizing "model" and argued that it is as a model of good practice that "represents an attempt to rediscover the 'social movement' origins of labor, essentially by redefining the union as a mobilizing structure which seeks to stimulate activism among its members and generate campaigns for workplace and wider social justice" (Heery et al. 2000a, 996). Associated with this is a range of techniques or methods that are designed to raise the profile of the union and encourage members to become active in union building rather than remaining as passive recipients. In a survey of UK unions mapping the very early adoption of ideas about organizing into the United Kingdom (Heery et al. 2000a), we reported that union organizers frequently used person-to-person recruitment, workplace mapping, the identification of workplace grievances, and the principle of like-recruits-like in their campaigns. However, we noted that less use was made of visits to nonmembers' homes and links with community organizations, which are more generally associated with union organizing in the United States (see table 1). What was notably absent in that early evaluation—and a theme we will return to throughout this book—was a discussion of the broader political ideas that had been evident in some discussion about organizing in the United States and other contexts.

This early evaluation of the Organising Academy and New Unionism within the United Kingdom showed very patchy adoption of core organizing tactics even in unions that had committed considerable resources to employing and training organizers. For example, table 1 shows that only 21 percent of unions had a policy to establish organizing committees in

TABLE 1. Some techniques and methods associated with organizing

Organizing techniques and methods	UK unions reporting frequency of use (%)
Person-to-person recruitment at the workplace	69
Raising the union profile within the workplace (through petitions, surveys, etc)	45
Identification of employee grievances as a basis for recruitment	34
Establishing membership targets at company or workplace level	29
Reliance on the principle of like-recruits-like	26
Establishing an organizing committee within target workplace	21
Systematic rating of nonmembers in terms of their propensity to join	7
Public campaigns against antiunion employers	5
Link-up with community organizations	3
House calls to nonmembers' homes	2

Source: Heery et al. (2000a), Survey of Union Policy and Practice 1998; unit of analysis = individual union; N (number of unions) = 61–64.

their targeted workplaces. Yet the need to leave behind sustainable lay organization after professional organizers have withdrawn from a campaign was already evident by that time and had been identified as an essential "exit strategy" if members were not to rely on negotiating, bargaining, and representation services provided a full-time official (Markowitz 2000). What is also clear from table 1 is that in the early days of specialist organizer training there was relatively little effort to apply a "bundle" of tactics together.

What was also absent from most of the early literature and practitioner debate in the UK context is any discussion of the wider purpose of organizing. Beyond a very generic idea of renewal and revitalization, there was little discussion of the core ideas discussed above. It is therefore important to reflect on contested implications of the purpose of organizing activity, as these tensions continue to reverberate in the analysis of impacts of organizing that we present in later chapters.

What Are We Organizing For?

As already highlighted, it is possible to identify a number of interrelated themes about the purpose of organizing activity within existing literature in the United Kingdom and elsewhere. First is a view that organizing activity is related to efforts to increase union membership. One reason for this position is to increase bargaining leverage at company or sectoral level. So, for example, Lerner (1992) presents an articulate defense of the view that high membership density is related to the ability of the union to take effective action on a range of issues. Specifically, he uses experience of and evidence from the US Justice for Janitors campaign to argue that sectoral density and bargaining strength are the central tenets of a strategy for taking wages out of competition and improving terms and conditions across a sector. He argues that this is the only feasible way to engage in a form of what we would in the past have called industrial democracy. In other words, Lerner (1992) argues that only through sectoral- and industrial-level union density can workers wield any wider democratic influence over their working lives. Thus increased membership is seen as a way to improve the ability of the union to regulate the employment relationship more effectively.

But this is not the only argument that supports increased union membership as a central objective of organizing activity. Also important is the contention that to support their claim that they are the representative voice of working people, unions must ensure that they are genuinely representative of the diversity of workers. Here the argument is that union organizing should focus on increasing membership among particular groups of workers that have been underrepresented in the union movement in the recent past. Specifically, some argue for the importance of targeting young workers (Waddington and Kerr 2008, Bryson and Gomez 2005). Others focus on black and minority ethnic (BME) workers (Holgate 2005, Perrett and Martínez Lucio 2009) or workers on atypical contracts (Heery 2004, Heery et al. 2004, Walters 2002). Still others stress the importance of recruiting workers in particular sectors such as private-sector services (Dølvik and Waddington 2004). It is important to note that these aspects intersect in important ways in the UK labor market; young, BME, and atypical workers are all more likely to work in private-sector service workplaces where unions have historically found it difficult to organize. There are multiple reasons for this historic difficulty in organization, but increasing evidence indicates that it is not primarily explained by negative attitudes of these groups of workers toward unions (Kirton 2005, Walters 2002, Bryson and Gomez 2005). A more convincing explanation of the lower union density among these groups is the structure of work and employment in the private service sector and, in particular, the dominance of small workplaces (Gall 2007). Thus the emphasis of these debates has tended to focus on how unions can effectively target organizing activity to facilitate higher levels of membership among these groups. However, this raises questions not only about how these groups can be targeted for membership but also about whether and how they engage with the democratic structures of unions.

For this reason, most writers and practitioners agree that organizing activity is more than simply a recruitment drive. At the most basic level, this is prompted by a recognition that if unions want to target underrepresented groups for membership and/or to build density, they have to have an increased presence in workplaces with little or no history of trade unionism. Within the UK context, if unions are to be influential in regulating employment at workplace, professional, sectoral, or even national levels, they must be engaged in collective bargaining. This requires formal recognition from employers, and in practice, for many unions gaining recognition is the central objective of their expansionist organizing campaigns. Because of the voluntarist tradition of UK labor relations, recognition for collective bargaining is not always granted through a legal process. Usually, it is simply a formal agreement with an employer that collective bargaining will take place. A recognition agreement will typically include explicit terms about the coverage (whose terms and conditions will be negotiated), the scope (what issues will be negotiated), and the pattern (how frequently bargaining will take place) of union activities. It may also include an agreement for representatives to take paid time off to undertake union duties. But unless a recognition agreement is secured through the statutory recognition processes, the form of these agreements is entirely at the discretion of the two parties. Thus there is a high degree of variation about whether particular roles are (and should be) taken on by workplace representatives or paid officers, and in workplace representation structures in general.

In the sense that organizing activity encourages membership engagement with the union at the workplace level, some have argued that organizing can be viewed as a strategy for wider union renewal rather than simply a tactic for increasing membership (de Turberville 2004, Simms and Holgate 2010a). Indeed Fairbrother (1996, 2000a) has consistently emphasized the importance of workplace activism in union renewal efforts. Again, however, notions of union renewal are contested. For some authors, the most important evidence of union renewal is increasing membership activism (Stinson and Ballantyne 2006, Kumar and Schenk 2006). This would be seen in increasing member self-organization, typically at the workplace level, and members taking greater responsibility for addressing workplace issues without officer support. For others, evidence of more extensive member engagement in democratic structures (Sciacchitano 2000) is the key measure of organizing "success" or "failure." A further element of this argument, frequently presented by those who focus their attention on the importance of unions increasing membership among underrepresented groups, is that organizing activity can and should target the engagement of specific groups of members in democratic structures. This is particularly clear among authors who discuss women's involvement in unions (Colgan and Ledwith 2002a, 2002b). Although women workers are proportionately represented among union membership, they are underrepresented in the decision-making structures of unions. Thus there are those who argue that if organizing efforts do not attempt to address this, unions are likely to become increasingly irrelevant to women within contemporary workplaces.

Finally, a clear strand of argument can be seen emerging in the US literature in particular, and this highlights the wider objectives outline above. Ideas about (re)building a form of "social movement unionism" (Buechler and Cylke 1997, Clawson 2003) or "community unionism" (Dunn 2010; Holgate 2009b; McBride and Greenwood 2009; Tattersall 2006, 2010) are evident in some discussions of union organizing. In practice this tends to mean developing formal and informal links between unions and other social justice campaigns to improve workers' rights. This implicitly accepts a more radical view of the role unions can play in social change and promoting social justice that may conflict with some of the more institutional and regulationist objectives discussed above. In the United Kingdom, there is relatively little evidence of this kind of organizing objective, although this view has been most closely associated with "community unionism" (Wills and Simms 2004, Wills 2004, Holgate 2009a, 2009b), which focuses on increasing the links between the workplace and the wider community, and on recognizing and building on workers' roles and connections beyond their workplace. What is important here is that the focus of such organizing activity extends far beyond any immediate improvements in workers' terms and conditions (although these may accrue from such activity), and that union attempts to become relevant to workers' lives means moving beyond a workplace, industry, or sectoral level.

These debates about the objectives and purpose of organizing activity highlight why we think it is so problematic to talk about an organizing "model" in any practical sense. We therefore avoid that term and focus throughout the book on exploring, understanding, and explaining the tensions that emerge between different ideas about what organizing "is" and what it is ultimately "for." The debates and discussions highlighted above help to inform the key themes and questions that link the different chapters.

Themes and Questions

Clearly then, ideas relating to the objectives of organizing activity are highly contested among both practitioners and academics. In this book we focus on one particular initiative—the establishment of the TUC Organising Academy—which was of central importance in expressing and promoting a particular shift of policy toward expansionist organizing activity, building membership in areas where unions were already recognized for collective bargaining, and advocating greater involvement by members and activists. By taking the establishment of the academy training program as the focus of our analysis, we can see the ways in which this training promotes particular approaches to trade unionism. We then trace the work of the graduates of the program to examine the extent to which their presence has acted as a catalyst for change toward the objectives outlined.

But it is important that we do not condense the story of organizing over the past decade simply to the TUC Organising Academy. We want to consider the broader impact of organizing in a UK context. What are unions doing when they run organizing campaigns, and what do they seek to achieve? What resources and tactics do they commit to these goals? How do employers respond to organizing campaigns? And what outcomes are there? By asking these questions, we aim to present a flavor of what organizing is "like" in the United Kingdom, which emphasizes deep differences between the United Kingdom and other countries such as the United States and Australia where much of this work has previously been done (Reed 1990, Foerster 2003).

We also take a look at the big picture in order to reflect on some of the wider changes we have seen across the union movement. What impact has the academy had on the labor movement more generally? How has the practice of training specialist organizers spread and developed since its inception? How have unions changed in that time? And what mechanisms for training other groups have been developed? These wider measures of the impact of organizers and organizer training give us a much more rounded view of the changes that have taken place since the late 1990s. The story is mixed; there have been some areas of notable success, and other areas where change has been slow and difficult. We explore these patterns and seek to explain them.

Structure of the Book

We want to reflect on union organizing initiatives in Britain since the mid-1990s. We start by giving a brief background to the central debates and arguments that have emerged around organizing. We are very keen to locate our academic work firmly within practitioner debates as well as academic debates. Inevitably some issues have exercised trade unionists far more than academics, and vice versa. Some of these discussions we have increasingly good evidence about; others less so. We are not trying to produce a definitive overview of all the debates around union organizing across the world. What we want to do in chapter 1 is to highlight key themes that set up our evaluation of organizing policy and practice in British unions so that we can then return to those themes and make a clear statement about what we think has happened since the start of the Organising Academy, which broadly coincides with the period of the New Labour government in the United Kingdom.

So why have we taken the period of New Labour (1997–2010) as our time frame? Clearly unions organized before this time, but in the mid-1990s there was a concerted effort by the TUC and by some senior national officers within unions to reject the consensual politics of "partnership" and to encourage investment in organizing. We therefore start our analysis by considering the national strategies that have been adopted and by explaining the TUC's role in promoting organizing activity through the Organising Academy and related initiatives. In chapter 2 we argue that the academy's relevance stems not only from its success in training a cadre of organizers—the majority of whom are still employed within the union movement—but also that its establishment promoted a debate about the central role of organizing within British unions. We describe and evaluate the training program and examine some of the ways in which its core ideas have spread through many British unions.

In chapter 3, we look at the spread of organizing ideas in more detail to evaluate how those ideas have changed, developed, and have been adapted to fit specific contexts. In doing this, we want to locate the activity of workplace union campaigns within a broader analysis of the importance of sectoral pressures, union histories and ideologies, employer responses, and the like, and to be clear about why we are doing this. It is not to privilege national activity and coordination; indeed we argue later that a balance between worker activism and leadership support for organizing is essential for effective and sustainable organizing. Rather, the aim is to begin with a picture of initiatives that have been important in securing resources for organizing activity, before focusing on the work that actually makes a difference at the workplace. Unlike some authors (most explicitly perhaps Bramble 1995), we think that there is an important role for coordinating organizing activity at the national scale. We will argue that, whereas these national initiatives have done very little actual workplace organizing, they have developed and promoted a context within which organizing campaigns can take place more effectively. We also agree with Martínez Lucio and Stuart (2009) that these national initiatives have provided important "narratives" for union renewal that help underpin and coordinate workplace organizing. Equally, we should be clear that we are not saying that there is one "best" way of doing this. What we see when we look across the British union movement is a breadth of organizing strategy and a diversity of practice that we could barely have imagined a decade ago. Many of the issues we describe and analyze here are highly contested and still subject to lively debate within the union movement. Individuals and unions disagree on the appropriate way to manage organizing activity; indeed, they often disagree on what organizing is and what they should be seeking to achieve through their organizing activity. A core theme of our analysis is that since the mid-1990s, there have been changes and developments in organizing ideas and practices, and we reflect on these, the motivations for them, and the consequences for the union movement and membership growth.

In chapter 4, we introduce the work of organizers—who they are and what they do. As specialist actors in the process of organizing, their training and experiences of work tell us a great deal about how organizing is managed and focused in British unions. They are at the sharp end of the difficulties and tensions inherent in trying to manage a cultural shift in unions toward organizing activity. They have competing and contested views about how these tensions can and should be addressed, and they are, in general, a highly reflective group of practitioners. We are therefore interested not only in the work that they do, but in what that tells us about how British unions are approaching organizing. We are interested in their challenges, stresses, and dilemmas, as well as the victories and failures because these tell us a great deal about how tensions are managed. In this chapter, we are particularly keen to give voice to these workers because their experiences of organizing are so central to the developments and initiatives on which we are reflecting.

In chapter 5 we look at organizing campaigns. Given that all union organizing activity must at some point engage with workplace concerns and must engage workers at that level, it is essential that we look at the processes involved in this endeavor. In this chapter, we engage the notion of workplace activism, and we argue that although it is essential that workers are actively involved with their union at the workplace and other levels, there is an important role for the kind of strategic coordination mentioned previously. We argue that workplace organizing alone is not sufficient to promote union renewal in Britain, although it is a necessary part of that process. In this chapter, we also engage with the responses of employers to organizing campaigns. Employer behavior is very often left out of descriptions and analyses of organizing activity, and this, we argue, is a mistake. We can often only understand the behavior of unions, workers, and organizers in the context of the behavior of employers. We therefore want to explain why employers are often resistant but not unrelentingly hostile to unionization in the United Kingdom, and why some employers are in fact supportive. Our central argument here is that the outcomes of union organizing campaigns, and therefore of the impact of organizing activity more widely, can only be understood within a much broader evaluation of the purpose, strategies, and context in which they take place. The competing views about the purposes of organizing activity can often lead to organizing strategies that have multiple, contested, and sometimes contradictory objectives.

In the final chapter, we step back from looking at specific issues and campaigns to evaluate the consequences of organizing activity across the union movement. Although the story that we tell is complex, contentious, and occasionally ambiguous, we can, nonetheless, generalize about broad trends and directions. It is absolutely clear to us that there is more organizing activity taking place within British unions now than there was when the academy was launched in 1998. Lessons have been learned (often the hard way—by losing cases, by failing to mobilize workers, and by having to back out of resourcing campaigns), and those lessons inform present practice. It is also clear that, despite problems gaining reliable financial data, unions are investing more in this kind of work. There is a cadre of people within the British union movement who regard organizing as central to the work they do. They are vocal and reflective, and many of them are becoming increasingly influential. In this sense, "critical mass" has developed that is changing—albeit slowly—what many unions do and how they do it.

The story, however, is far from universally optimistic. Union membership has stagnated even in the broadly favorable political and economic conditions of the past decade until the financial crisis of 2008. Employment grew strongly across the British economy but unions largely failed to recruit and organize in these new areas. As a result, density levels have declined at an aggregate level, but as we shall see, this masks distinctive sectoral and industry patterns that are not as gloomy as the overall picture suggests. The period of economic and fiscal challenge, since the financial crisis of 2008, presents even more serious difficulties. It is unclear whether unions will be able to take advantage of their sectoral and industrial position to negotiate wage increases in the coming period. It seems unlikely that governments in the near future will actively support the right to statutory union representation or to the statutory imposition of collective bargaining. Overall then, our evaluation comments not only on what unions have achieved under New Labour but also on the position that leaves them in to weather future storms. In summary, our view is that unions have done much to change themselves in the past decade and that they are probably better placed than they were, but very serious challenges remain.

1

FROM MANAGING DECLINE TO
ORGANIZING FOR THE FUTURE

The steady decline in British trade union membership from 13.3 million in 1979 to 7.2 million in 1996 led the Trades Union Congress to launch the New Unionism initiative, not only to provoke a debate on how to revive the future of trade unionism but also to provide guidance and support to unions on developing new renewal strategies. As highlighted in the introduction, New Unionism was far broader than just a focus on organizing. It was a broad-based effort at using a range of strategies to promote revitalization. So, for example, the development of the Organising Academy sat alongside an almost simultaneous development of a Partnership Institute that promoted cooperative relations with employers in the hope of winning mutual gains. The apparent contradictions between these initiatives led to significant debate, particularly within the academic community (Carter and Fairbrother 1998, Heery 2002, Badigannavar and Kelly 2011), although some practitioners were more relaxed about the implications. John Monks, then general secretary of the TUC, argued that the position should be to organize "bad" employers and develop partnership arrangements with "good" employers. What is important is that the discussions about union renewal in the mid-1990s clearly located organizing efforts within a much broader context of the political, social, and economic challenges facing the UK labor movement.

That there has been a turn toward organizing in the UK union movement since the mid-1990s is undisputed, but the extent to which organizing works—that is the extent to which new organizing approaches are able to reverse the decline—is more contentious. In part, this relates to the reasons why the decline occurred in the first place and the balance of class forces ranged against the union movement during the growth of neoliberalism. Academics and practitioners have been debating these issues over the years and keen observers of the union movement will be familiar with the many arguments and counterarguments put forward to explain the social, political, and economic factors influencing the way unions and their members (or nonmembers) behave. These debates have been wide ranging—many have extolled unions to organize their way out of the these challenges (Cooper 2000) while others have adopted a more pessimistic tone (Machin 2000, Disney 1990), arguing that economic forces are the determining factors influencing union growth and power and that, despite best intentions, union organizing initiatives, while potentially beneficial in small-scale individual workplace campaigns, have little effect in significantly increasing overall membership growth. The aim of this chapter is to review some of the main debates in the context of the changes experienced in the British union movement over the last few decades and to understand what implications different economic, political, and social factors have had on the development and adoption of union organizing approaches. There is little doubt that unions faced an increasingly difficult social and economic context during the 1980s and 1990s and that in many cases the factors affecting union membership have continued. The fallout from the economic and fiscal crisis of 2008 will affect people for decades to come and we can be sure that it is likely to hurt the working class much harder that those who have sufficient capital to ride out the economic downturn. But if it is true that union growth is dependent on external factors like these—many of which are beyond the immediate control of unions—why is it that organizing activity has become of such central importance within British unions?

Debates have raged about the relative impact of the different causes of the persistent decline of unionism from the peak of 1979, and it is often difficult to disentangle them (see Simms and Charlwood 2010 for a fuller discussion). The economic, political, and social environments in which unions are operating have become significantly more challenging with, among other things, the decline of the manufacturing sector where union membership was strong. Further, the growth and diversity of service work has been associated with a growth in the workforce in sectors and jobs that have not previously been unionized (personal services, professional services, among others) as well as large numbers of small workplaces that unions have traditionally found difficult to organize. At the same time, the profile of working people has changed. The increasing feminization of the labor force (and union movement) has challenged many of the structures and patterns of interest representation within unions, and despite the changing gender demographics, union officers and activists still reflect the "pale, male and stale" image of yesteryear. This is despite female union membership overtaking male membership in Britain, such that 54 percent of union members in Britain are now women (Office for National Statistics 2010). Similarly, the growth in the migrant labor force, while not as dramatic, has also caused unions to refocus their organizing work to bring in these new workers, many of whom are working at the margins of the economy and subject to considerable exploitation (Holgate 2011, Perrett and Martínez Lucio 2009). In this chapter we explore some of the many arguments put forward by academics and practitioners for the factors influencing union decline and the possibilities for union growth, before moving on to highlight the tensions and debates that are raised as a consequence of the kinds of developments outlined.

Economic and Technological Change

Many economists and industrial relations scholars have argued that union strength and activity is primarily affected by changing economic circumstances and that unions are, to a greater or lesser extent, recipients of membership rather than active agents. Some authors (Bain and Elsheikh 1976, Bain and Price 1980) argue that membership levels are more influenced by factors beyond the control of unions such as the level of inflation, real earning, and the level of employment. From this perspective, there is little unions can do to reverse a membership decline when these wider forces are against them. Without doubt, recent decades have seen an increase in global trade and rapid changes in the use of technologies, which have had many implications for product and labor markets. While it is difficult to disaggregate the relative effect of growing trade and technological change on labor relations issues such as union membership and power (although see Freeman 1995 for a discussion), we can say is that the effects of these developments on the context within which unions operate have been profound.

In short, increased product and service competition usually makes it more difficult for organizations to pass on any rises in labor costs to the end user. As a consequence, it can be more difficult for unions to gain improvements in terms and conditions. Mobilization theory (Kelly 1998) helpfully illustrates how this shifts the cost-benefit judgment for workers in taking collective action. It also gives employers a sound reason to try to reduce the influence of unions within the organization. By and large, increased international competition makes employers more vulnerable to rising labor costs in relation to other international competitors. It also undermines the logic of national level multiemployer collective bargaining, which was a common strategy to help unions take wages out of competition in the United Kingdom until the 1980s. Technological changes (especially the use of information and communication technology in service work, and the automation of factory work) make it easier for employers to substitute labor with capital and to intensify work. In the UK, these changes have particularly affected factory workers doing routine but skilled work (Autor et al. 2003, Goos and Manning 2007) and possibly lower-skilled workers (Machin 2001) who formed the bulk of trade union membership until the 1980s. This has been disastrous for UK unions as these skilled manual workers were previously the ones who were most able to win improvements to their terms and conditions because of their hard-to-replace skills and traditions of collectivism learned through the apprenticeship system. Taken together, these developments present significant challenges to unions in building collective solidarity and achieving economic benefits for workers. But it is not only the economic context that has been changing in recent years; the institutional context has also been considerably transformed.

Changing Institutional Context

The study of the institutional arrangements within which the employment relationship takes place is one of the core principles of industrial relations

(Edwards 2003). It is therefore unsurprising that there has been a long tradition of explaining union behavior in terms of the structure of collective
bargaining and other aspects of the wider institutional context such as legislation. The impacts of policies of national governments and suprana-
tional institutions such as the European Union (EU) on union membership
strategies have been closely studied (for example, Freeman and Pelletier
1990). An important way in which government policy can affect organizing activity is by promoting an environment that is hostile to or supportive of trade unions in general. Freeman and Pelletier (1990) identify the
law as an essential determinant of the industrial relations "climate." The
first point to note is that the institutional context of British labor relations
shifted dramatically in the 1980s, with seventeen consecutive years of Conservative Party dominance of UK politics. During this period, most notably associated with Margaret Thatcher who led the Conservative Party for
much of this time, a series of laws were introduced that constrained the
ability of trade unions to take collective action. These included, but were
not limited to, the introduction of laws similar to those in "right to work"
states in the United States through the abolition of closed shop arrangements, constraints on the range of issues over which unions can take collective action, strict rules about conducting a postal ballot of all affected
union members before industrial action can take place, the requirement
to inform the employer one week in advance of any industrial action, and
harsh penalties for any breaches of the law. Even before the election of the
Labour Party in 1997, Tony Blair was clear that these laws would remain
in place, and indeed they are in place to this day.

Smith and Morton (2001, 2006) argue that the New Labour governments developed a distinctive form of neoliberalism with regards to employment legislation. Specifically, the continuity of the Conservative Party
restrictions on collective action was combined with "a more subtle dis-
course of social partnership and collective and individual rights" (2006,
414). In practice, although most unions are now familiar with the legal
requirements of industrial action and have become used to working within
this legislative framework, taken as a whole, the law places very real constraints on workers' ability to take effective industrial action, and this has
a number of impacts on union organizing activity. First, it places serious
"costs" on the side of the "cost-benefit" decision of both the decision to
unionize in the first place and of taking industrial action once the union

is established. As a consequence, this can constrain the likely effectiveness of unionization in the United Kingdom. Second, this legislative program was one aspect of a very real institutional shift of power toward employers over the 1980s and 1990s that helped to delegitimize unions in the wider sociopolitical context.

Despite a continued commitment of the Labour Party to many of these legislative initiatives, there have been some important changes. Most observers agree that since the election of the 1997 Labour governments the legislative context has become a little more sympathetic to trade unionism than under previous Conservative administrations (Oxenbridge et al. 2003, Undy 2002, Gennard 2002). The introduction of a raft of European Union employment legislation, the national minimum wage, and most relevant here, the introduction of statutory recognition procedures in the Employment Relations Acts of 1999 and 2004 promoted an environment more conducive to trade unionism, which triggered unions to engage in organizing campaigns (Gall 2004a). The statutory recognition legislation put in place a mechanism by which unions can, in principle, compel employers to bargain if the majority of workers want the union to represent them. Smith and Morton (2006) argue that these laws in fact enshrine the illegitimacy of unions because unions are only given very limited rights under very strict conditions. Nonetheless it is, we argue, important that such legislation exists at all and concedes a role for collective bargaining; something that was generally not accepted by Conservative Party legislation and social policy from 1979 to 1997.

Legislation is only one way in which the institutional context can facilitate organizing activity. Industry-specific policies may also create an environment that makes organizing activity more or less attractive to unions at particular times; for example, the economic policies that were pursued throughout the 1980s and 1990s that led to a decline in the British manufacturing sector. The extent to which these policies have intended or unintended consequences on opportunities for union organizing is not immediately relevant here. The point is that government and employer policy often interact to create an environment in which union organizing becomes more or less difficult. We are particularly keen to include a consideration of employer behavior in the analysis we present. Specifically, we want to look at how the "success" or "failure" of many organizing policies and practices rest not only on the behavior of the unions themselves but also on the behavior of employers and other institutional actors. And in setting ourselves the task of evaluating the impact of organizing initiatives over the period of the New Labour governments, we feel it is important to integrate this institutional analysis.

Clearly all of these factors influence the context within which unions organize, and they also influence union decisions over which groups of workers to target in organizing campaigns. One of the most significant challenges for unions over the past decade or so has been the increasing diversity of the UK workforce and the interests they bring to the workplace.

Increasing Diversity of Worker Interests

All these factors have created a context within which it is increasingly difficult to identify a homogenous "working class" in the way that was once thought to exist (see Crompton 2008 for an extensive discussion). An obvious example in relation to trade unionism relates to the changes in lifestyle (declining relative cost of and increasing access to transportation and patterns of house prices, for instance) that mean that workers often no longer live close to their workplace. As a consequence, their experiences outside work are increasingly different from each other. There is less of a common physical geographical community that ties workers to place or lived space. As such, local collective identities are harder to establish and maintain. Together with the increasingly diverse demographics of workers and the increasingly wide range of jobs they do it can be very difficult for unions to identify and construct a coherent, shared set of interests around which to organize. This has led some commentators to emphasize the need for unions to develop new and innovative organizing strategies to respond to the changing and increasingly diverse workforce (Healy et al. 2004b; Holgate 2004a, 2004b).

Although gender is by no means assumed to be the only way in which workforce heterogeneity exists, it is the area where there has been most research and debate and is therefore the area where theoretical contributions are most developed. The growing participation of women in the labor market during the past forty years has brought with it debate about the extent to which women have similar or different interests to men. Many authors have examined the ways in which trade union agendas can privilege male workers (among many others Cobble 1993, Colling and Dickens 2001, Cockburn 1991) and have argued that women can bring different issues and interests to trade unionism, for example, a greater interest in flexible working patterns (Conley 2005), maternity provision, or even, a less confrontational way of negotiating (Hurd 1993). Although the precise nature of these proposed differences and the ways in which women can more successfully have their interests represented has been hotly debated, the key point here is that these authors all argue that to some degree there is divergence between "men's interests" and "women's interests" and that unions that build gender-specific organizing strategies may be more successful in their organizing work (see Hurd 1993, for an example of how gender-specific organizing tactics were used during the Harvard University clerical workers campaign).

Similarly, the issue of how best to recruit and organize black and other minority group workers has been an important part of the ongoing debate within union and academic circles (Humphrey 2002).[1] The British trade union movement's response to the involvement of black and minority ethnic (BME) workers within its ranks has not always been positive and, in some cases, despite official policy statements in opposition to discrimination, it has been objectively racist in practice (Phizacklea and Miles 1987, Radin 1966). There has, at times, been an unwillingness to recognize the racism experienced by black workers, leading some black union members to believe that trade unions do not adequately represent their interests (Bradley 2002b, BTUSM 1983, WEA 1980). Only since the late 1970s, as a consequence of challenges from black activists and antiracists, have trade unions been forced to reevaluate their so-called "color-blind" stance, whereby they regularly asserted that there was "no difference" between BME and white workers (CIR 1974, CRE 1985). The importance of these contributions is that not only do they not assume homogeneity of worker interest, but they argue that homogeneity is neither achievable nor necessarily desirable. In the area of union policy, for example, this discussion is perhaps most evident in Unison's development of "self-organized groups." Unison, the largest public-sector union covering the UK, has developed formal self-organized structures (black, women, disabled, lesbian, gay, bisexual, and transgender) throughout the union, from national to branch level, all of which are able to create and influence union policy (see McBride 2001 for further discussion).

---

1. The term *black* has been adopted by UK trade unionists to describe radicalized minority ethnic groups. It is used in a political sense rather than a description of skin color.

However, the idea of self-organization is not without controversy. In the beginning, there were claims and counterclaims that it was separatist, divisive, and distracted from the main goals of trade unionism. As a response to the inaugural meeting of one union branch's black self-organized group, 219 white members signed a letter objecting to its establishment: "We the undersigned...express our outrage...[the Black Workers Group] can only be viewed as divisive and offensive and is surely a retrograde step in the area of racial harmony at work...stop it now" (Virdee and Grint 1994, 221). Yet self-organization has continued to develop in UK trade unions and has functioned relatively well despite the "backlash" anticipated by some union officials. Many long-standing black trade unionists believe that the development of self-organization had had a huge impact on the trade union movement since the 1980s, creating space for black activists to play a role in their union, which otherwise would not have been possible. As an example, 80 percent of respondents to a questionnaire survey at the TUC Black Workers Conference in 2002 stated that BME structures were important in providing space for BME union members to get involved in their unions, where they might otherwise be excluded. This is also borne out by recent research into black women activists in trade unions, where it is reported that self-organized structures are a "critical means of voicing a collective experience and are a means of harnessing a collective black voice in the union" (Bradley et al. 2002a, 20). The main point made by the foregoing authors is that that the diversity of interest of these groups means that unions may need to develop particular organizing strategies to target them effectively, which may include the employment of union officers that represent the workers targeted for organizing campaigns. While this may not be particularly surprising to observers of sections of the US union movement, it is only since the development of the TUC Organising Academy that the British trade union movement's officer corps has become more diverse and has utilized the organizing practice of "like recruits like" (Holgate and Simms 2008).

Building Solidarities

As a consequence of these developments, some authors inject a note of pessimism in their evaluation of the prospect of large-scale organizing success, because the context in which union organizing now operates is so challenging (Gall 2007). The combination of increasingly diverse worker interests, increasing heterogeneity in skills requirements, experiences of work, and increasing rationale for organizations to avoid unionization undoubtedly places significant challenges in the way of workers seeking to organize. But we argue that it is extremely problematic to think about union membership as purely a function of external forces operating on unions. We argue that unions do have some degree of agency and are able to influence membership levels through the choices they make.

Despite these challenges, other commentators are more optimistic that unions can at least construct collective solidarities even within this difficult societal and economic context. In contrast to many authors, Hyman (1997, 1999) explicitly acknowledged this throughout his writing on worker interests. He argues that the notion of worker interests rests on "imagined solidarities" that have traditionally privileged the interests of one group of workers (skilled, white, male, full-time, manual workers) above others (unskilled, ethnic minority, women, atypical, and service workers). Yet because he emphasizes the extent to which "through their own internal processes of communication, discussion and debate—the 'mobilization of bias'—unions can help shape workers' own definitions of their individual and collective interests" (1999, 96), he is relatively optimistic that unions can therefore "reimagine" collective interests to reflect the changing interests of a changing workforce and membership.

Further, developing the work of Fantasia (1988) and Gamson (1995), Kelly (1998, 30) also acknowledges the extent to which this process is socially constructed but focuses on the importance of leaders and activists in attributing a sense of injustice and creating social identities ("us" as opposed to "them"). In his writings on mobilization theory and its applications within the field of labor relations, Kelly (1998) stresses that, under certain circumstances, groups such as unions can be extremely effective at facilitating the process whereby workers attribute grievances to managers and collectivize in order to address those grievances. However, Kelly emphasizes that there is a process of making "cost-benefit" judgments about the likely effectiveness of collective action. If there is little chance that collective action will be successful in addressing grievances, or if the costs of collectivization are so high as to be punitive (for example, by workers losing their jobs), these potential outcomes may well act as a constraint on collectivization.

What is particularly important about the work of both Hyman (1999) and Kelly (1998) is that they emphasize the ways in which the processes of building solidarities and collectivism are socially constructed. In other words, solidarity and collectivism do not simply exist—and, importantly, never have existed—independently of the work done by interested parties (here, trade unions, but traditionally also including political parties and other interest representation groups). Trade unions have been at the forefront of deciding whose interests are legitimately represented in campaigns and bargaining. And in promoting those interests above others, a feedback loop is created through which members and potential members receive important messages about whose interests are legitimately represented by those unions. These viewpoints offer reasons for optimism for union renewal; unions have some degree of agency in their destiny. They can choose which interests to represent and diversify those interests as the workforce becomes more heterogeneous. However, it is a view that also raises very serious concerns about the extent to which unions are able to do this in practice and how they should go about this considerable task.

Debates about Interest Representation

Union strategy, policy, and practice are central to understanding how and why unions behave in the ways that they do. We are keen to consider the ways in which internal union structures and governance influence organizing activity. It is particularly important to reflect on these debates, because as highlighted in the introduction, a central idea within organizing relates to the objective of developing increasingly participative forms of trade union governance.

Most existing literature identifies two different perspectives on how organizing activity can be planned and undertaken. On one hand centralized leadership may drive a professionalization of union activities (including organizing), which emerges because of the scale of the challenge facing unions seeking to build new solidarities and new collectivisms. This contrasts with an alternative view, which tends to promote the importance of rank-and-file activism that facilitates and encourages members to access the resources needed to solve their own problems. Fairbrother (2000b) identifies this as a distinction between the "principle of leadership predominance" as compared to the "principle of membership participation." These two perspectives suggest different approaches to organizing activities within union structures; the first emphasizes union leaders in promoting such activity and renewal, and the second emphasizes union members in promoting organizing activity.

For example, Kelly's writing on mobilization theory (1998) identifies a clear role for leaders in the process of collectivization. Kelly's argument is that leaders are important for four key reasons: they help construct a sense of grievance among workers, they promote group cohesion and identity, they urge workers to take collective action, and they need to defend collective action against claims that it is illegitimate (Kelly 1998). These arguments privilege the contribution of leaders and union structures in the process of organizing, mobilization, and renewal more widely. They are united by the theme that organizing activity will originate from innovative leaders, usually officials, and that these leaders are best placed to make decisions about renewal efforts as they have the necessary skills and expertise to take a broad view of the strategic direction of the union. This contrasts with others, most notably Fairbrother (1989, 1996, 2000b), who place much greater importance on the role of workplace activists in promoting and instigating organizing activity and who are also argued to be the key to long-term union renewal. Fairbrother is a particularly important author as he argues that the changing political and economic environment makes workplace union activity crucial by demonstrating the effectiveness and relevance of unions to workers who may have little previous understanding of what unions do. In one paper, he even goes so far as to stress that "renewal is about the way unions reorganize and recompose themselves to meet the problems of work and employment...it is in the workplace that unions organize, sustain and renew themselves...any move towards union renewal must and will come from the bottom up" (Fairbrother 1989, 3, 4, 6). On the subject of union leadership, he argues that leadership turnover is a prerequisite for renewal (1989, 25) and that the process of renewal may be actively resisted by union officials (1996) who seek to perpetuate bureaucratic union structures. In several places, Fairbrother makes the case that leaders from the central union structure may resist attempts at renewal, including organizing activity if that organizing activity threatens their power bases. Fairbrother's arguments are important because they explicitly marginalize the importance of union structures outside the workplace in promoting organizing activity and renewal more broadly. Further, he views these structures as potentially limiting the opportunities for renewal, arguing that organizing efforts that do not originate from workers will fail to reflect the problems that workers encounter and therefore, ultimately, fail to renew and revitalize trade unions. But his work focuses largely on renewal in workplaces where unions are already established, and he makes little comment on how unions might seek to expand into new areas of representation.

What both perspectives tend to share is an acknowledgement that, no matter who promotes it, workplace activism is crucial for building successful organizing activity and that some kind of coordination is needed to make that happen. So it is worth emphasizing that the debate is largely one of emphasis rather than absolutes. This is important because it helps move us beyond a fairly sterile debate between those arguing for leadership or membership dominance in the way organizing is promoted and delivered. The importance of a more nuanced discussion is emphasized in work by authors such as Voss and Sherman (2000) who argue, based on a study of organizing activity in local US unions, that the support of the central union leadership is crucial in leading to full revitalization of union locals. They go as far as to point out that the process that led local unions to initiate organizing campaigns was "not one of bottom up, local innovation that later reached the top echelons of the bureaucracy....Rather, progressive sectors of the international exerted varying degrees of influence over locals in crisis, which led to full revitalization" (2000, 337). Grabelsky and Hurd (1994) also emphasize the importance of leadership in ensuring that existing union policies and structures are challenged. Quantitative data from the United States also stress the association between leaders promoting union innovation and more effective organizing outcomes (Fiorito et al. 1995). In the United Kingdom, authors studying TUC initiatives such as the Organising Academy have focused on the role of union officials in managing and promoting the process of transformation (Heery et al. 2000a), arguing that managing the process of organizational change is crucial to broader renewal.

These contributions all emphasize the importance of union structures, policies, and practices in promoting organizing activity at the workplace level, which is regarded to be the locus of union renewal. At first glance, this literature appears somewhat contradictory. It is firmly rooted in an acknowledgement of the necessity for strong grassroots activism yet argues forcefully for the importance of the role of union officials in promoting this activism; what has been described elsewhere as "managed activism" (Simms 2007a).

The important concept here is of "articulation" of objectives and activities between different levels of the union (Waddington and Kerr 2000, 259). What links these authors is their emphasis on the central union structures creating frameworks (which may be communicated in a range of ways: for instance, written policies, training programs, and rewarding particular behavior) within which local unions can organize effectively. These frameworks ensure that local unions have adequate skills, resources, and support to organize outside their existing membership bases. Local unions can, in turn, draw on the support of the central union to legitimize their organizing activity to existing members who may see such activity as too risky, too innovative, or as diverting resources from existing members. Further, the central union can provide a source of ideology, values, and language to legitimate potentially risky organizing activity at lower levels of the union (Batstone et al. 1977 write most extensively on the ways in which this process of value formation can occur). From this perspective then, the role of central union leadership in promoting organizing activity is crucial.

Some work has tried to reconcile the apparent contradictions in this literature and develop the argument of the importance of strategic (as opposed to opportunistic) management of organizing activity. The notion of "managed activism" (Simms 2007a, Heery 2003, Jarley 2001) simultaneously emphasizes scope for unions to build strong membership-led (what is more consistently, although less elegantly, referred to as "bottom-up") organizing campaigns while coordinating strategy and structural change from the center. These authors recognize the importance of paid officials in allocating scarce union resources to key functions (including organizing) and recognize that this is a contested process. They also emphasize that newly organized members may not have the necessary skills to represent themselves effectively and that unions may need to develop these skills through training.

We can clearly see that there is considerable debate about how union organizing activity emerges, but also about the desired outcome of organizing. At first glance, this appears to be a debate between those arguing for a participative "bottom-up" form of organizing, as against those arguing that there is a need to coordinate and manage this process. But this rather simplistic analysis hides considerable debate about the purpose of organizing activity and the objectives that unions should consider when planning and developing organizing strategies. What emerges, therefore, is the need for a more nuanced analysis of the tensions (and, perhaps, contradictions) within the processes of planning, promoting, and delivering organizing activities.

Two Key Questions: Power and Democracy

Underpinning this summary of the literature and themes of current debates are two centrally important ideas: (1) the extent to which unions are (or are not) able to renew themselves so as to increase the degree of power they exercise in the labor market and in society more widely, and (2) the role of internal union structures in that process. In order for us to differentiate between different kinds of organizing outcomes, we need to be clear about different ideas of union "power." Union power is a remarkably undertheorized area of labor relations, and yet it is essential to evaluating organizing activity and is very often taken for granted by both trade unionists and academics. Early theorists writing on power (French and Raven 1960) differentiate between coercive power and legitimate power. This is a particularly useful differentiation when it comes to thinking about labor unions and where they derive sources of power. Coercive power is, in essence, the power to get someone to do what you want them to do because the alternative would have a cost or some other negative effect on them. Unions use coercive power when they threaten to take industrial action, when they threaten to give an employer bad publicity, or when they "harm" an employer in some other way. But threats only work some of the time and labor unions have to build open-ended relationships with employers that are not based on threats most of the time; thus, they need legitimacy in the eyes of both employers and workers, and if they can establish legitimacy in the eyes of policymakers and politicians, so much the better although the latter is not essential.

Reading about and listening to ideas around organizing in the United Kingdom and elsewhere for much of the past decade, it is clear that both trade unionists and academics are often very confused about what they want unions to achieve by investing in and promoting organizing. In our view, this is because they are often confused about the extent they are hoping that organizing activity will increase a union's legitimacy power or the extent to which they hope it will increase the coercive power. Different approaches to organizing can achieve either, but they are likely to emphasize one over the other and in some ways this is linked to the earlier debate about organizing and partnership.

Most researchers and practitioners accept that organizing is about more than simply building union representation—that its objective is to revitalize and renew trade unionism at workplace level and beyond. This requires membership engagement in wider decision-making structures. This approach to organizing emphasizes members taking responsibility for identifying and resolving workplace issues through mobilization, collectivization, and activism. Union structures, it is argued, must change and adapt to encourage this and to become more responsive to a member-led movement (Carter 2000). From this perspective, the purpose of organizing activity is not simply to establish trade union representation in workplaces where there was previously none but to initiate a transformative process that may have consequences both for workers and for unions.

This is why we think the issue of union democracy has become so problematic in some writing on organizing. Lerner argues that "if only 10 percent of workers in an industry are unionized, it is impossible to have real union democracy because 90 percent of the workers are excluded" (cited in Crosby 2005, 741). For him, the central union must take control of organizing unorganized workers across, for example, a sector or industry, even if that means going against the views of existing members as expressed through union elections and other democratic processes. While recognizing the validity of this point, Crosby (2005, 741) takes a different view and acknowledges that issues of democracy have been problematic in US discussions of union renewal. He argues that "democracy has been both fetishized and trivialized in the current debate." He is highly critical of the view that union democracy is an impediment to building powerful unions and that union elections divert resources away from the agenda of organizing for density across sectors. Crosby (2005) rejects this view entirely. To him, it fails to differentiate between workers' control over their jobs (linked to union density) and workers' control over their own organizations (through union elections). Crosby argues that both are equally important and that a central objective of union organizing activity is to revitalize union democracy as well as to secure bargaining effectiveness through high density.

In short, the themes of the extensive research highlighted in this chapter speak to important questions about how unions seek to strengthen their different forms of power through organizing activity. Research into organizing activity has the potential to transform internal structures and participation to improve the representativeness of unions. These themes reappear throughout the following chapters and are crucially important in our overall analysis of the impact of over a decade of organizing activity in UK unions.

2

The TUC Approach to Developing
a New Organizing Culture

We want to start our evaluation of UK experiences of organizing by looking at the attempts by the Trades Union Congress to promote and develop organizing from the mid-1990s onward. Of course, we are not suggesting that organizing did not exist before then. Rather, we believe that the New Unionism initiative and the related development of the Organising Academy represented a turning point in ideas within the UK union movement about how renewal and revitalization might develop. One of the central objectives of the academy was to recruit and train a new cadre of people to work in British unions. The academy training is an intense and challenging experience for the participants, and it is designed to equip them with the skills not just to become organizers but to promote a particular approach to trade unionism in general, one that emphasizes membership participation and activism. This sometimes brings academy graduates into conflict with other people within their own unions, and it raises questions about how union work should be organized and managed and the extent to which organizers have an input into union organizing strategies. Many of these tensions are played out in the day-to-day jobs undertaken by organizers and their responses to these challenges are often informed by their training, typically delivered through the TUC Organising Academy program. We start, therefore, by considering the origins of the Organising Academy and the training program itself. What training do organizers receive, and how does it differ from that of generalist union officers? How do organizers evaluate the OA training, and how useful and appropriate has it been to them in the jobs that they have gone on to do? In chapter 4, we then pick up on how the nature of organizing training and work affects organizers in their day-to-day lives in both the professional and personal realms. It is also interesting to note that this heavy emphasis on training has a clear normative influence in encouraging the legitimacy and diffusion of organizing practices and is analogous to professionalization processes noted more generally in studies of developing professions (DiMaggio and Powell 1983). The importance of training as a process to develop and embed professional norms has been underlined by the development of organizing training for both officers and activists. This is important because, as we shall see, organizers very often see themselves as being at odds with the dominant culture of the unions in which they work. They often express loyalty to their professional identity as organizers as much, if not more, than identification with their employing union. We discuss this idea more in chapter 4, but here it is sufficient to flag the central role in shared training in instilling these ideas.

Origins of the TUC Organising Academy: The Transfer of Ideas from the United States

Starting our story with the development of the TUC's organizing training program highlights how in the United States, Australia, and now the United Kingdom, national union confederations have often taken a central role in the diffusion of ideas and practice of organizing at important moments. It also illustrates how ideas have spread within and between national settings. The American Federation of Labor–Congress of Industrial Organizations (AFL-CIO) and Australian Council of Trade Unions (ACTU) have both championed organizing unionism nationally and contributed to the international spread of ideas and practices associated with organizing. It is without doubt that the TUC has explicitly learned from and mimicked developments in both the United States and Australia. Throughout 1996 and 1997, the TUC facilitated a series of visits by senior policymakers within the UK labor movement to both Australia and the United States to observe organizing training and initiatives underway. They also organized a series of conferences and visits by senior officers from those countries to the United Kingdom to explore some of the detail of what organizing might mean in the UK context.

Interviews with those key actors at the time highlighted how important those visits were to the development of the Organising Academy training program and to the ways individual unions implemented their own policies. Interviews that were carried out with the small group of officers and trainers who developed the Organizing Academy training program consistently refer to the influence of those experiences. One interviewee who was at the time the senior officer responsible for organizing in a small industrial union explained how before he had visited the United Steel Workers of America (USWA) in 1997 his union had intended to hire just one organizer to place on the Organising Academy. After that trip he argued for five trainees and was keen that they were fresh to organizing. He was very impressed by his time spent working alongside a "young lass [woman] from Organizing Institute who had big, hairy-arsed steel workers eating out of her hand" and became convinced that if new recruits were as enthusiastic about organizing as he was, their age and gender would not prove an insurmountable barrier to their organizing efforts. Interestingly, one organizer who worked within the unit during his training year noted the potentially more negative side of this approach to organizing.

> [Name of officer] had been to America, so he'd seen these kind of young kids fresh out of Uni, sleeping on floors, travelling thousands of miles across the Continent. So I think he thought that [could be done in the UK.] I think that's probably why he took me on actually. And I think it was quite hard. I suppose I didn't really have the guts to say at times "This is a bit unreasonable." Or "What's being expected isn't really on." (OA organizer #67, white male)

The underpinning ideas of the academy are modeled on similar training institutions that have been set up in the United States and Australia, the Organizing Institute and Organising Works respectively. From the outset, it was clear that the way in which the TUC was championing organizing was a break from the past, and promoting organizing unionism has emerged as an important new function (see Heery, Simms, Simpson, et al. 2000). In particular, the influence of experiences from those trips to the United States was in evidence with the very "hands on" approach taken by key figures in writing the training material. One of the people responsible for developing and delivering the academy training in the early stages noted in one of our interviews that the idea that the training might promote a particular approach to organizing was a radical departure from the traditional role of the TUC. "[The idea that] this is the best in a kind of evangelical way went against their [the TUC's] basic principle of being nondirective."

Since the very early stages of developing organizing training in the UK, overseas visitors have played significant roles as speakers, advisors, and trainers. Events such as conferences focusing on organizing and debates at conferences have, in aggregate, exposed a substantial proportion of UK union activists and officers to the ideas, language, and techniques of organizing. This interaction across the international field of confederations is continuing with interest from other countries, including Denmark, Ireland France, Germany, Austria, Sweden, South Africa, and Zimbabwe. Because of this international influence, it is necessary that we lay out and explain some of the ways in which organizing ideas and practices are similar to and different from those seen in other countries. Our focus here is on the United States and Australia as these are the two countries that had already set up training programs for specialist organizers by the time the TUC developed an interest in this. It is also notable that these were the countries that were used as points of comparison by practitioners and policymakers themselves.

The Influence of the United States and Australia

Others have written extensively on US industrial relations (Turner et al. 2001), so our objective here is simply to point to the key factors that allow us to understand the development of the particular philosophy of union organizing that has become so influential in the United Kingdom. Three factors strike us as particularly noteworthy in explaining how and why organizing in the United States is so different from the United Kingdom: collective bargaining structures, the dominance of the closed union shop in US unionism, and the particular influence of the anarcho-syndicalist ideology promoted particularly (although not exclusively) by the Industrial Workers of the World (IWW). The first two are closely intertwined. Collective bargaining structures in the post–New Deal context rest largely on securing recognition for bargaining at the level of individual workplaces. Thus, it is common in the United States that some workplaces of a large company may be unionized while others will not be. Further, for much of the post-1945 period, there has been a substantial union wage markup that typically gives unionized workers rights: for example, to employer-paid health insurance, better holidays, and other benefits (Wheeler 2002). The union wage premium, combined with an assertive managerial culture, ensures that there are strong incentives for employers to resist unionization. Alongside this, most states have a system of post-entry closed shops, whereby all workers employed in that location must join the representative union. This secures income for the union from member dues.

Together, this structure of trade union membership and collective bargaining informs a clear logic of organizing at the workplace level. Within this context, organizing activity largely focuses on prerecognition work, that is, persuading workers that a union could effectively represent their interests if they collectivized. Unions know that this kind of intensive work with rank-and-file activists will not have to continue after recognition because once recognition is secured, officers of the union can negotiate and renegotiate the contract, terms, and conditions at predetermined intervals (servicing). Identifying activists during the prerecognition phase is essential because much of the day-to-day representation work will be done by these activists. Teaching workers to act collectively is also crucial because these are the skills that they will be expected to use to ensure that the negotiated contracts are being enforced. Face-to-face recruitment in the workplace or in workers' homes is essential in a context where membership numbers matter and access to workplaces prior to recognition is extremely limited. A claim for recognition is highly likely to end up being assessed by the National Labor Relations Board (NLRB), which will look for evidence of membership as the key indicator of the strength of support for the union. So having organizers who can "sell" the union—typically through their own experiences of unionization—is central to the success of a certification campaign.

What is usually less explicit within US analyses is the "business union-ism" inherent in some ideas of "classical organizing," specifically, the idea that, ultimately, paid union officers have responsibility for bargaining once recognition has been secured (usually through NLRB processes). This has often had the effect of disempowering workers from some of the emphasis on collective action that can develop during a lengthy recognition campaign (see Markowitz 2000 for extensive case studies). Throughout the 1980s and 1990s, "business unionism" came under increasing pressure and was fre-quently identified as a key reason for the decline in union strength in the United States, prompting both academic and practitioner debates to seek alternative visions for the trade union movement (Bronfenbrenner et al. 1998, Turner et al. 2001).

Alongside this kind of workplace-focused organizing—described by Craft and Extejt (1983) in an early paper as "classical organizing"—a par-allel notion of organizing reflecting the influence of the IWW has persis-tently been evident in US debates, particularly on the left of the trade union movement. Understanding the influence of the IWW on US ideas about organizing is essential as it helps to explain why "organizing" became an explicitly political rallying cry throughout the 1980s and 1990s. This sense of organizing as politics by and large has been lost as debates about or-ganizing have transferred to the UK context. The IWW takes an essen-tially anarcho-syndicalist position on labor relations, which emphasizes worker self-organization. Although the IWW has always been a minor player in US labor relations, their influence on debates—and most par-ticularly on the left of the US union movement—is undoubted (Kimeldorf 1999). IWW ideology emphasizes the importance of worker collective ac-tion at the workplace level and rejects the idea that paid union officers take responsibility for bargaining once recognition was secured. For the IWW—in common with many syndicalist positions—the objective of or-ganizing activity is to use the tactics described above to ensure that workers have sufficient skills and knowledge to continue to organize and represent themselves, often, ultimately, with the objective of presenting a fundamen-tal challenge to structures of capital accumulation. Collective bargaining may be temporarily advantageous in redistributing wealth, but it is only one small part of the objective of organizing activity. As such, organizing across workplaces is of fundamental importance to ensure sufficient "industrial" power, and the core of the IWW position remains a focus on continuous worker self-organization.

Although there is evidence of a long history of debates about organizing activity, and especially debates over the *purpose* of organizing activity, within the US labor movement, throughout the 1980s and 1990s unions were faced with a particular conjunction of factors that explains why a more leftist vision of "organizing" shot up the agenda of the US labor movement. The end of the Cold War, the crisis generated by collapsing union membership figures, the growth of union busters and the associated difficulties getting recognition cases through the NLRB process, and generational change within individual unions and within the AFL-CIO allowed much freer discussion on the American left about the future of the union movement and strategies for renewal (Bronfenbrenner et al. 1998, Mort 1998).

This vision of organizing goes far beyond Craft and Extejt's (1983) description of "classical organizing" tactics and integrates elements of the more syndicalist view of workplace self-organization (although it rejects the revolutionary undercurrent of the IWW position). But by the mid-1990s, one essential factor had changed: the political context of unionism and union organizing. Prompted by some of the wider changes mentioned above, in 1995, John Sweeney won the election to the leadership of the AFL-CIO under a campaign entitled "New Voice," which put a central emphasis on the importance of organizing work. This signaled a very substantial move in US union politics, although one that inevitably had its roots in previous developments. Politically, this was a shift away from the Cold War politics of Sweeney's predecessors (the comparatively conservative eras of Meany and Kirkland) and a definitive shift to the left. Sweeney himself came from the Service Employees International Union (SEIU), which had developed influential and innovative organizing campaigns among low-skill service workers throughout the 1980s and 1990s and explicitly moved away from the business unionism of the Cold War era.

It was precisely at this point that, prompted by many of the same crises of membership decline, UK policymakers became very interested in US developments (Simms and Holgate 2010a). While practices associated with organizing transferred to the UK, many of the political ideas that can be identified within US approaches to organizing are absent. The central political and practical contrast at the time was between "organizing unionism" and "partnership unionism" (Heery 2002). In the UK, interest in union organizing as a separate, specialist function emerged in the mid-1990s largely as a reaction against some of the practical and political criticisms of the "new realism" approach that promoted ideas of a consensual "partnership" with employers. Around that time, key policymakers at the TUC and in affiliate unions became interested in US programs such as the Organizing Institute and Union Summer, which were explicitly intended to attract young people, ethnic minority workers, and women workers to work within the union movement. Importantly, these initiatives were also underpinned by ideas of worker self-organization and were explicitly linked to the political agenda of shifting the culture of US unions away from "business unionism" toward "organizing unionism."

Although some—but by no means all—senior figures responsible for launching and steering the TUC's New Unionism initiative and Organising Academy accepted that the politics of worker self-organization underpinned their vision for a future direction of the union movement, these objectives were rarely, if ever, explicitly stated. Further, unlike the AFL-CIO, senior positions within the TUC are appointed, not elected. Thus, there was never a need to build a political campaign around a vision for union organizing. Indeed, precisely the opposite. Some senior TUC figures were highly aware of the political underpinnings of ideas about organizing but saw that the way to encourage adoption of organizing policies was to discuss practices and tactics rather than the broader political agenda. Given the decline of influence of trade unions in the 1980s and 1990s, few within the TUC or affiliate unions could effectively argue against tactics that might attract members, whereas a broader debate about the objectives of those tactics may well have entrenched political resistance. Unsurprisingly, therefore, within the UK context, the primary interest became to promote a set of organizing practices that would encourage unions to engage in membership growth activities. Further, the introduction of organizing ideas alongside the ideas of "partnership" (i.e., relations with employers intended to pursue mutual gains) meant that from the very early days of the New Unionism initiative there was a very different dynamic in the United Kingdom to the ideas against which organizing counterposed itself (Heery 2002). Taken together, this meant that the effect was to shift the debate away from the *political* objectives of organizing, and toward the *practice* of organizing.

One interviewee who is a senior officer with responsibility for developing organizing policy illustrated this point.

> It's almost like the problem with the Organising Academy—not the problem—but one of the issues is that almost you reduce organizing to a set of organizing techniques rather than what is this actually about. It's about changing the way that unions work and about changing the relationship between unions and the members. And there's a danger that it just becomes, it's about workplace mapping, identifying and developing activists, issue based campaigning. Well it's all those things but that's—they're techniques, that's not a coherent ideology. (Interviewee #20, white male)

We argue that there were several important consequences of shifting the focus away from the *politics* of organizing toward the *practice* of organizing. The first, and in our view most important, is that any notion of there being a single "model" of organizing has been abandoned in UK unions. To support this, in the following chapter we present evidence of the implementation of organizing practice in three large UK unions over the last five years that show significant divergence in both practice and the underlying purpose of organizing activity. We argue in later chapters that, as a consequence, there is a lack of coherence about the purpose of organizing activity. We develop these ideas later in the book, but it is important to keep them in mind as we explain how and why the training has been developed in the ways that it has and the ways in which it influences the people who go through it.

Phase One: The TUC Organising Academy Training

The Organising Academy has been the flagship program of the TUC's New Unionism initiative to renew the UK union movement. It is a one-year program where trainees work in a sponsoring trade union, interspersed with blocks of three or four days residential training. Around 240 trainees graduated in the ten years since its launch in 1998. The intention was to train specialist organizers who could work within their unions to promote change and renewal. In part, it was hoped they would do that by focusing attention on recruitment and organizing, but it was also intended that as they became more experienced and confident, they could push unions to develop strategies and policies that were conducive to organizing activity. There was an explicit intention to try to recruit people with campaigning experience, but not necessarily those who would traditionally have found work as union officers. It was hoped that they would generally be younger and more diverse than the established officer corps and bring with them knowledge of campaigns from outside the union movement.

In many respects, the academy has been successful in achieving these objectives. Our evaluation of the program in 2008 showed that the recruits are notably younger and more diverse—particularly in terms of their gender and ethnicity—than the established officer corps. For many of them, the Organising Academy presented a way of entering into employment in a trade union that would not have been open to them otherwise; perhaps because they did not have sufficient experience, or perhaps because the union's rules required a certain amount of time served as an activist within that union. The academy has been less successful at recruiting people from outside the trade union movement. The vast majority of trainees have had experience as activists within a union, although, notably, not necessarily within the union that then sponsors them. In chapter 4, we introduce far more evidence and discussion about the lives of these organizers, what they do and what they think about their work, so we will come back to a much deeper discussion about the trainees and graduates as agents of change. Here we simply want to introduce some demographic background about the people who chose to become the new generation of union organizers. We found the answer to this question by contacting 191 graduates who had completed the training program between 1998 and 2008 and for whom we established contact details. We asked them to complete a lengthy survey and very kindly, 133 (70 percent) obliged. This was a good response and one that included graduates in each year's intake. Sixty-eight respondents were female and 65 male, and their ages ranged from twenty-one to fifty-nine, with the majority clustering around the age range thirty to forty. Ten percent of the respondents were from black and minority ethnic groups, lower than the TUC had hoped, but nevertheless a welcome increase in the diversity of trade union officials.

Organising Academy graduates are well-educated workers, with 49 percent having an undergraduate or postgraduate university degree and another 21 percent a further education qualification. In all, the academy seems to have been largely successful at recruiting a cadre of organizers who are younger and more representative of the working population than the officer corps had been previously. What was perhaps most striking about the previous experience of academy organizers was the breadth of roles they had prior to starting their training. For a few, it was their first job after graduating from university, while others had ten to twenty years' work experience. Some had worked in factories, in retail, and waitressing, and others had previously had professional jobs in both the public and private sectors—working for local government or the civil service, in journalism or voluntary sector organizations. The range of roles is so varied that it is impossible to generalize about the type of jobs from which organizers originate. However, what is more consistent is their experience of unions prior to their training. Fewer than one in ten had no previous engagement with unions and around three-quarters of them had held some kind of formal lay representative role in their workplace. This is particularly noteworthy given the ages of the organizers; predominantly union members in their twenties and thirties. Clearly, they are atypical of workers this age, both in the sense that they are highly aware of union issues, and that they are keen to be actively involved in their unions. What is also evident from their previous experience is that they were not, in the main, coming from the existing ranks of union staff officers. Although 10 percent said they had previously worked for a union, only two had been full-time officers prior to starting their academy training.

As noted, three-quarters of graduates had been activists in one form or another, and they reported that this had been important in prompting them to want to deepen their involvement. Interestingly, 42 percent said that they had previously held a formal role within their lay branch representative structure, indicating that many of them were highly familiar with how the more formal aspects of unions work. Of those who did not have previous experience with trade unions (around 10 percent of the cohort), most were recruited to the Organising Academy directly from university. Many of them had been active within the National Union of Students, or had campaign experience around environmental issues or in charity-based organizations. This is not especially surprising, as a background in either union campaigning or other forms of campaign work is essential to succeed at the selection process for the training program.

Since 2005 there have been two routes into the academy: either through the TUC selection process or through a direct process arranged within individual unions. Prior to 2005, all graduates were selected through the TUC. The direct route is typically only open to candidates who want to work in the union where they are already activists. This route allows some unions (for example, Unison) to identify and "fast-track" their own activists to the academy. Whichever route is chosen, applicants must demonstrate familiarity with issue-based campaigning, project planning, and broader issues of social justice. Applicants are assessed by senior organizers from the sponsoring unions, based on a set of agreed criteria, and this is done at a two-day Development Centre, where applicants are given an intensive range of tasks working with other applicants. If they pass this stage of the selection process, the short-listed candidates are then placed into a pool and are invited to interview by the sponsoring unions. Successful applicants from both routes are then offered a one-year, fixed-term contract for the duration of the training and although the trainees are formally employed and trained by the TUC, the sponsoring union pays their salaries.

There have been some important changes in both the content and delivery of the program. For example, at the outset, the plan was to deliver the residential program through a network of experienced trainers. It quickly became apparent however that this was problematic, in no small part because of the lack of organizing experience of these trainers. Logistically, this presented the TUC and the sponsoring unions with a significant problem: there were comparatively few experienced organizers within the UK union movement who had the appropriate training skills. It was therefore extremely difficult to find staff that had the necessary experience and credibility in the eyes of trainees. Eventually a small number of key staff were seconded to deliver the training over the first few years, but their roles as organizers meant that they were keen to return to their primary jobs rather than to become professional trainers. Over ten years on, finding staff with appropriate skills in both organizing and training remains a significant challenge for the academy because most organizers wish to either continue working as specialists or to become generalist officers. The approach taken more recently has been to use the skills of a number of key trainers (often in that small group of organizers who do wish to move into this role) employed specifically to run the academy and deliver the training. Other experienced organizers are seconded to the program to deliver individual sessions or exercises. The challenge with this approach is that it is highly dependent on a small number of staff.

In addition to staffing decisions, a further strategic challenge has been whether or not to deliver the training as an "in-house" TUC program. Despite the cost to the TUC, there was initially a strong preference for this approach. Until 2005 the TUC largely ran the academy using its own resources. However, this arrangement became increasingly untenable since 2005 when the TUC closed its training center and changed the structure of its education and training provision. Since then, the training has been delivered in partnership with a further education college, Newcastle College, which has allowed a number of significant developments. One of the considerable attractions of delivering the training in partnership with a college is that it allows the program to become accredited for the purposes of continuing vocational training. This ensures that the program is part of the national postcompulsory education system and is recognized as a formal qualification by prospective employers. To achieve this accreditation, the program has to be verified by external bodies, and there are formal, relatively bureaucratic requirements relating to the ways in which learning objectives are identified and assessed. All programs seeking access to public funds must, unsurprisingly, demonstrate that there are clear and appropriate intended learning outcomes, that there is a structure of training intended to help students move toward those learning outcomes, and that there is appropriate assessment about whether students have achieved those outcomes. This process is essential to secure access to public funding that is available to all accredited courses run through appropriate training colleges such as Newcastle College. Access to this funding is very helpful for the Organising Academy as it means that it is no longer an expense entirely borne by the TUC. It has also meant that the program has had to become far more structured and formalized than in the early years.

This shift was acknowledged by key respondents with responsibility for the transfer of the program to the accredited college:

> The money comes from the Learning Skills Council. To do that you've got to have a learning aim so the course has got to be accredited to actually draw funding....[Before] they [tutors] just turned up and [taught] a class and that's fine.... We have put a lot of work in in the past two years to get a proper curriculum, proper lesson plans, schemes of materials...and

learning outcomes so that we know what we are working towards. Because previously that didn't exist.[1] (program director, Newcastle College)

What we have seen as a consequence is both a quantitative and a qualitative change in the training experience. Quantitatively, the number of training days has been reduced considerably, from thirty-five in the first year, to sixteen, and back up to twenty in 2008. This has been prompted by a desire to focus the content on the "core skills of organizing" and is also informed by the process of formalization and application for funding described above, which has clear guidelines about the number of hours of contact time between tutor and student that is appropriate for different levels of qualifications. What these figures on training days do not highlight, however, is a wider qualitative shift in the focus of the training. During periods of observation of the training, the contrast between the early years and more recent years is particularly notable. In the early years, the sessions were far more discussion based, very informal, and were intended to provoke trainees to reflect on and discuss strategic issues facing the trade union movement. They were immediately responsive to the discussions that had occurred, and frequently sessions for one day were developed overnight as a response to a particular discussion or line of enquiry from the students. Trainers (who were mainly experienced organizers) drew on their experiences to develop case studies or discussion materials very quickly. In later years, even though there has been an effort to maintain some of this approach, there is a great emphasis on ensuring that trainees write down their reflections on the subject at hand in order to demonstrate that intended learning outcomes have been achieved. Sessions are far more structured, and there is evidently a curriculum that needs to be covered in a particular time frame. Largely as a result of this, there has been a notable shift toward reflecting on and assessing organizing practice, rather than the more conceptual and strategic discussions that happened in previous years. Clearly it is impossible for us to know the exact content of every discussion in every year of the academy training, but as observers who

---

1. Learning Skills Councils are a now defunct way of allocating public funds for postcompulsory education and training. They administer the process of evaluating whether the learning outcomes are appropriate and are being assessed appropriately. They then allocate funding to accredited programs.

have sat in on training sessions, it is very notable that there has been a shift to more skills-based training rather than discussion of the strategic or theoretical issues relating to organizing.

This is an important shift that has considerable consequences for organizing activity more broadly. For example, focusing on the core organizing skills that are transferable within most campaign contexts means there is less opportunity for debate, discussion, and exploration of some of the more strategic issues associated with this kind of culture change program. Returning to the argument outlined in the previous section of this chapter, it is clear that a combination of pressures has pushed the Organising Academy training to teach a set of key skills (a set of "tools") that are largely devoid of political or theoretical intent. When the training was originally launched, much of the gap between the practice and objective of organizing was filled by semistructured, classroom-based discussions about what organizing "means" in the context of different unions. Comparatively little of this is evident today.

The TUC officers responsible for the program defended this shift by emphasizing that the Organising Academy is often the first year of training for an organizer and should therefore primarily focus on the core skills. If an organizer then starts working in a union and wants to develop those skills into some of the more strategic aspects of the work, there are now training programs that allow them to do that which did not previously exist and which are discussed in more detail later in this chapter. It should also be noted that the residential nature of the blocks of training (two to three days at a time) means that there is plenty of time for more informal discussion over meals and in rest periods. Observation of the sessions in more recent years suggests that trainees do take these opportunities to discuss the broader purpose of organizing and what they may be seeking to do within their different unions. Indeed, as we shall show in chapter 4, they regard this kind of networking opportunity as essential to their professional development as *organizers* rather than as generalist officers. The point is that there is a lot less time given formally to discussing these issues.

The rationale for this change in emphasis is clear and is, in many respects, very useful for the TUC. The TUC explicitly tries to stay out of any kind of role that might be perceived as interfering with the day-to-day processes of running individual unions, and it would certainly be regarded as problematic if affiliate unions perceived that the TUC was trying to

TABLE 2. Effectiveness of organizing training
How would you rate the effectiveness of the training you received at the Organising Academy?

Outcome	Very ineffective or ineffective	Neutral	Effective or very effective
Improving your ability to:			
Identify organizing issues	3	8	89
Recruit new members	5	14	81
Plan campaigns	6	12	82
Identify new activists	5	12	83
Develop union organization	8	15	77
Solve organizing problems	9	18	74
Research organizing targets	12	30	59
Identify sites for organizing	10	38	52
Train other organizers	19	31	50
Deal with the media	19	30	51
Deal with employers	35	40	25
Improving your knowledge of:			
Organizing techniques	4	9	86
Organizing in other UK unions	17	29	54
Equality issues	20	29	51
Organizing in other countries	44	26	30
Employment law	37	37	26
Internal union procedures	37	39	24

Source: Survey of OA graduates (n=129–132).

impose any kind of political agenda from outside. But it nonetheless has an important impact on the training and the perception of the training expressed by graduates. We can see this reflected in graduates' responses to our survey questions that asked them about their satisfaction with the training. As part of the ten-year evaluation of the Organising Academy in 2008, we asked graduates about how effective they felt that their training as organizers had been. We asked about a range of different aspects of the program, and the questions and responses are outlined in table 2. We found that there was an overwhelmingly positive response to all of the questions. However, there was a difference between OA graduates' responses to the questions asking about the "core skills" of organizing such as recruiting members, identifying activists, and identifying organizing issues, and some of the more strategic aspects such as identifying sites for potential organizing campaigns and dealing with employers.

It really is important to emphasize the overwhelmingly positive response that graduates gave to these questions; on every issue apart from dealing with employers, over half said that their training was either effective or very effective at improving their ability to do these things. However, this table starts to give us clues to an emerging issue about the extent to which organizers are equipped to deal with some of the more *strategic* aspects of broader culture change, a theme that will be returned to in later chapters. We argue later that these more strategic aspects of organizing risk moving into a more explicitly political agenda about the *purpose* of organizing activity more broadly and that this has generally not been picked up by most organizing training and broader discussions in UK unions. We go on to argue that this limits the scope not only of what organizing is understood to be (a toolbox of practices) but also what its purpose is.

This is also evident at the bottom of table 2 where we asked about the knowledge-based (rather than skills-based) aspects of the training. Graduates were extremely positive about the effectiveness of the training in improving their knowledge of organizing techniques. However, on some of the other issues, many of which, such as employment law and equalities issues, are central to a broad-based effective implementation of organizing tactics, the scores are much lower. It is also perhaps surprising that only 54 percent of the graduates say that they felt that the training was effective at providing them with knowledge of organizing in other British unions, as a central objective of the academy training is to bring together organizers from different unions so that they can share their experiences. We suspect that this reflects the more practice-focused approach that we have highlighted. In other words, trainees might discuss similar (or different) practices being used in different unions, but that gives them little insight into what organizing really "looks like" in different settings.

Table 3 further develops this idea that the focus on more skills-based training may be a source of frustration for graduates. In an effort to tap into views about what graduates think should be the focus of the training, these questions asked about whether the focus of the training was judged to be appropriate. Again, questions relating to the appropriateness of the core skills training were very positive. But again, the more strategic aspects are rated notably lower—and sometimes much lower. In many respects, it is not surprising that graduates say that the training was largely ineffective at equipping them with skills to deal with employers; that is not a central part of the training, and it is a deliberate decision by the trainers to keep it separate from the academy training program. But table 3 shows us that

TABLE 3. Do you feel that the Academy training year gave/is giving appropriate emphasis to the following activities?

Activity	Too much emphasis	About right	Too little emphasis
Direct recruitment of new members	6	89	5
Recruiting activists	0	87	13
Promoting workplace organization	1	88	11
Promoting the organizing agenda	8	82	10
Planning organizing campaigns	2	82	15
Encouraging recruitment by activists	1	78	21
Identifying targets for organizing	5	66	29
Researching workplaces targeted for organizing	5	63	33
Training activists in recruitment	0	62	37
Preparing organizing material/literature	1	55	44
Representation of individual employees with problems (grievances)	0	52	48
Negotiation with employers over terms and conditions	3	40	57
Negotiation with employers over recognition arrangements	4	32	64

(n = 122-129)

Source: Survey of OA graduates.

50 to 60 percent of the graduates feel that it would have been helpful to have this as part of the training.

What is perhaps more surprising from this data is the clear message that a significant minority (between around 30 to 40 percent) of graduates feel that there was too little emphasis on skills that might easily be considered to be central to organizing activity, but which are more strategic than some of the core skills such as recruiting members and identifying activists. So, in the middle of table 3, we see a range of questions relating to identifying organizing targets, researching target workplaces and employers, training activists in recruitment, and preparing organizing materials, which are all important organizing skills within a broadly defined idea about organizing activity. This is strong evidence that supports our observations of a shift away from discussions and debate relating to the more strategic aspects of organizing and culture change. We go on to argue in later chapters that this presents significant challenges to the broader objectives of culture change within British unions.

Overall, however, the academy graduates spoke extremely positively about their experiences during the training. In our interviews with them, they were almost evangelical about the experience. They spoke positively about the opportunity to exchange ideas and experiences with other participants and the opportunity to think through particular challenges with people who had similar experiences, but who were working in different contexts. One graduate summed this up with a specific example:

> It was really useful. There were parts where we would have people come in from other unions talking about campaigns they'd run, ideas they had, and stuff like that I think was the most valuable. When you actually got people doing the job and doing something, I think they had the guys in from [a particular campaign] to give us a presentation one time. I remember that…it stands out in my mind as being really useful beneficial thing to actually hear from these people, how they did it. And the challenges they had and how they overcame them. And I think that out of all the training actually hearing from real case studies was really good. (OA organizer #39, white male)

The most common substantive criticism about the training was precisely the issue about the transferability (or not) of core organizing skills and the extent to which the different contexts in which organizers were working was formally recognized in the training. The organizer just quoted picked up this point: "I think there needs to be perhaps some recognition that unfortunately different people, different professions do have to be organized in very different ways. And I think there's perhaps not quite enough recognition of that, or certainly there wasn't in my experience" (OA organizer #39, white male). Another linked the point to some of the broader issues around the political objectives of organizing more generally: "I don't think it geared people up for really organizing on the ground. I think because it had to cater for so many unions politically in terms of what they wanted organizing to be, I think it ended up being a compromise too far actually" (OA organizer #24, white male).

These quotations raise important points that we will develop and expand on as we discuss the wider implications of the development of organizing and, in the final chapter, attempt to evaluate the impact of the "turn" to organizing. The important point to note here is despite the fact that graduates are, overall, very positive in their evaluations of their experiences at the academy, this hides an important criticism about the comparative lack of emphasis on some of the more strategic (and, we will go on to argue, political) aspects of organizing.

Phase Two: Organizing Training for Officers

In light of these issues, it is important to note that the second phase of the development of the TUC Organising Academy has been to create an organizing training program for generalist officers, and phase three intends to do something similar for lay union activists—discussed in the following section. One senior official noted that the purpose of this training was to try to move toward a notion that organizing activity should be more integrated into the day-to-day work of officers: "I think increasingly what we're trying to do as a union is to make sure that everyone is trained in the organizing side and has that awareness from the full timers [generalist officers] who come perhaps from a more traditional route" (OA organizer #39, white male). In order to achieve this, the TUC and many of the affiliate unions have developed a much broader range of organizing training programs for generalist officers. A TUC officer responsible for this innovation explained how much of his work is related to developing bespoke programs for individual unions; some of which, like Unison, have had little formal engagement with the Organising Academy. For him, this represents a very real commitment on the part of these unions to engage with organizing debates and to try to work out what kind of training and investment would be appropriate for them.

In addition, Newcastle College has developed an online module called "Why Organize?" which is targeted at generalist officers and which can be done entirely through internet-based learning. Interestingly, this is a development of an existing two-day training program that has been targeted at officers but which had comparatively few enrollments. The online delivery method has significantly increased the registration, with sixty people enrolled in the course in the first year (2007). The flexibility that is now built into the program through the change of delivery means that more and more people within the union movement are being formally trained in organizing skills.

As the director of the program at Newcastle College explained, this was always one of the attractions for them in running and delivering the academy training. Expanding to deliver a wider range of organizing courses in an increasingly diverse range of delivery methods is an attractive source of funding for the college. This marks a significant departure from the early justification of the need to train primarily specialist organizers. Indeed in 2004, in an attempt to deal with the issue of cultural change within unions, the TUC launched a program called "Leading Change," which is targeted at senior policymakers who have the power and resources to effect change within their organizations. In this program, there are five modules spread over twelve months, again with some residential commitment, some of which involves looking at overseas organizing initiatives in the United States. Of these five modules, two explicitly address organizing activity and the way in which strategic decision makers can facilitate a change of culture and approach within their own unions. Other modules integrate organizing activities within broader debates about the changing world of work, and this is an explicit effort on the part of the TUC to address the potential difficulties that can be presented by placing the responsibility for culture change on a small number of often relatively junior members of staff.

Phase Three: Training Lay Union Activists

Developing from the current thinking around the need to provide organizing training to the existing officer corps, a similar argument is increasingly being voiced about the need to train workplace representatives in organizing techniques and skills. The best estimate is that there are around 200,000 workplace representatives in the United Kingdom, and they are often the main or only face of the union at workplace level, but until fairly recently, specialist organizing courses have not been specifically aimed at this group of trade unionists.

In 2006 Newcastle College developed online modules aimed at lay activists and intended to develop organizing skills, but TUC figures for 2006 (TUC General Council Report 2007) show that only 637 activists were trained on TUC-delivered organizing programs that year, and that figure includes Organising Academy participants. This contrasts with 6,790 union activists who took courses in industrial relations and collective bargaining, and 6,225 who took courses in health and safety issues. A TUC memo highlights the likely reason for this disparity: "This low-take up is driven by a number of factors including the difficulty of securing employer time-off for training relating to organizing and recruitment. Another factor is that classroom based organizing training is likely to be of limited value unless it is linked to practical organizing activity in the workplace" (TUC memo 2008, 2). In an effort to address this low response to organizing training, the TUC has rolled out a program of training targeted at activists, with the intention that it should link classroom training and practical organizing work in a similar manner to the existing

Organising Academy. The program is usually run over a year, so that activists attend three blocks of intensive two-day training. The sessions are run at different times and in locations across the United Kingdom.

During the period of training, there is a structured system of support for activists to develop strategies and ideas about how to grow the union in their own workplaces. Support comes from tutors and from mentors who can either be more experienced activists, professional organizers, or generalist officers. The intention is that activists bring with them a campaign that they want to develop over their period at the Activist Academy. Typically this would be a workplace campaign, but it may be a regional or national campaign if that is more relevant. The objective is to work with activists to build their organizing skills and to strengthen their unions. It is important to note that the Activist Academy is a route into the Organising Academy with the intention of providing the opportunity to spot talented activists who might have the skills and enthusiasm to become professional organizers.

At the time of writing, the Activist Academy is in its early stages, and it is impossible to evaluate yet the impact it has had. What is important to note here is that it fills a very clear gap in the strategy and policies of both the TUC and of individual affiliate unions. It provides a relatively inexpensive opportunity for unions to develop the organizing skills and expertise within the union. However, an obvious potential weakness of the program is that it will require time to attend the training. Some activists may be able to negotiate this with their employers as part of their union duties, but in general in the UK "facility time," that is, paid time off for union duties, has been declining steadily in the past twenty years (Darlington 2010). It therefore seems likely that the majority of activists will have to choose to invest their own time to develop these skills. This is not inherently a problem; unions depend on the volunteered time of activists in order to survive. But it does start to indicate an argument that we go on to make more explicitly that there is a danger that this training will be focused in workplaces where the union already enjoys a comparatively strong presence. It is quite probable that activists in workplaces where the union is weaker will find it extremely challenging to run the kinds of projects envisaged in the design of the program.

Nonetheless, the development of the Activist Academy is an important step forward for the TUC and affiliate unions. It indicates investment and activity in a neglected and crucial area. Until now, the training of activists has been largely ad hoc and dependent on individual trainers and individual training programs in different unions. Inevitably there has therefore been a very patchy coverage of this area of skills development and capacity building, which is now being addressed in a more comprehensive manner.

Conclusions

Since the mid-1990s ideas about organizing have migrated from other countries, and from the United States in particular, into the United Kingdom. As those ideas have moved across national boundaries and into new institutional contexts, their meaning and emphasis has changed and developed. This chapter has outlined some of the main ways in which that has happened and some of the reasons why. Obviously it is impossible to capture the nuance and minutiae of what is inevitably a complex process. What we have tried to do here is outline the way in which the TUC led this process in what was a considerable departure from its previous role. In establishing the Organising Academy, the TUC developed a clear commitment to strengthening and expanding trade union membership after a period of significant and continuous decline since the late 1970s. But that commitment was only part of a much broader strategy that included potentially contradictory initiatives such as establishing mutual gains relationships with employers through company-level partnership agreements.

The key to understanding how and why the TUC was able to (and was keen to) pursue both approaches at the same time is to understand the ways in which ideas about organizing were not associated with any strong political philosophy or objectives. It is, to some degree, inevitable that those who took exception to the cooperative approach to employers promoted through ideas of partnership found a home in organizing. But it would be wrong to assume that there was a confrontational or radical approach to trade unionism *inherent* within organizing ideas as they transfer to the United Kingdom. Organizing transferred largely as a "toolbox" of tactics from which organizers can select as they see fit and to whatever ends they choose. Understanding this is central to understanding the issues we discuss in the following chapter where we look at the way in which organizing policy and practice has rolled out in individual unions. The main reason for this very particular view of organizing activity lies largely in the role of the TUC as an umbrella organization rather than a confederation that has policymaking powers over its affiliates. As a consequence, affiliates had to be free to take up organizing ideas in whatever way suited them and to whatever ends suited them. The TUC's role has been to provide training, develop networks, and encourage affiliate unions to make what they want of the resources available.

This has been a remarkably successful project in its own terms. The rating of satisfaction with the academy training by those who have undertaken it is strikingly high. In the period of our research approximately 240 trainees have graduated from the training program, and the vast majority of them still work in the UK trade union movement. Chapter 4 looks at their lives and experiences in some detail, but here it is sufficient to note that their impact on their employing unions has been profound. Together with the training of organizing specialists, the promotion of organizing ideas and the training of generalist activists and officers by the TUC has helped facilitate an environment in which it is now quite normal for UK unions to have clear organizing plans and strategies. In the next chapter, we will find out what those plans and strategies look like in individual unions. Here, the important point is to note the impact that the TUC-led initiatives have had on the UK union movement since the mid-1990s and the extent to which this was a move away from the coordinating role that the TUC had traditionally taken on.

However, that is not to say that the assessment is only positive. There are some very profound concerns over the (entirely logical) decision of the TUC to emphasize organizing as a "toolbox" from which organizers, officers, and activists can pick and choose tactics to whatever ends they wished. We will develop this theme in a more critical manner in the final chapter and emphasize that there are some profound weaknesses in seeing organizing only as a set of tools. One of those that has been highlighted in this chapter is that some of the more strategic aspects of organizing can get neglected in training, and consequently in how organizers, activists, and officers think about the purpose and potential of organizing. Another is that organizing activity remains largely targeted at workplaces where unions already have a presence because the "toolbox" of tactics can be more readily applied where there are existing activists and access to the workplace. Despite these weaknesses, the impact of the Organising Academy and the subsequent initiatives has been profound. Our attention therefore turns now to considering how these ideas have transferred into individual unions.

3

THE SPREAD OF ORGANIZING
ACTIVITY TO INDIVIDUAL UNIONS

This chapter looks at how organizing ideas and practices have spread beyond the TUC and into individual unions. In 2010, the TUC had fifty-eight affiliate unions. Some large unions are not affiliated to the TUC, most notably those that have a dual representation function both as a professional regulator and a trade union. These are mainly health service unions such as the Royal College of Nursing and the British Medical Association. Our attention here is on TUC-affiliated unions because these account for the bulk of UK union membership, and it is here that membership decline has been particularly problematic, thus focusing attention on renewal efforts.

A central practical question for unions that are thinking about how to manage organizing activity within their own context is the extent to which organizing is managed as a separate, specialist activity, or fundamentally integrated in the work of generalist officers. Different answers to this question reveal very different ideas about what organizing is in different contexts. Our research clearly shows that the idea of a single organizing "model" has never taken hold in the United Kingdom, largely as a result of the diversity of unions engaged in developing and participating in the Organising Academy and in organizing ideas more widely. The breadth of workers, sectors, and employers inevitably bring substantial complexity. More important, organizing in sectors that already have union recognition, but where some if not the majority of workers are not members, is extremely significant in the UK context. Although all of the participating unions have attempted to give their academy organizers opportunities to apply their skills in nonunionized sectors and workplaces, most organizers have focused on places where unions are still recognized for collective bargaining. This difference largely arises out of the fact that "closed shop" compulsory membership has been unlawful in the United Kingdom since the early 1990s, and also from the fact that so many UK unions organize within the public sector where union recognition is largely taken for granted. This has inevitably led to a much broader range of activities being defined as organizing within the UK context than, for example, in the US context. Reflecting this, in a presentation to the Working Lives Research Institute (February 20, 2008), Paul Nowak, then TUC national organizer, pointed out that one of the core objectives of his department in the coming years was to move away from the idea that organizing can present "off the shelf solutions to complex problems." Indeed, he identified what he called "organizing fundamentalism" as a danger because it suggested that a single model of organizing might provide a solution to all union ills. This chapter shows clearly how different unions have been able to take ideas about organizing and apply them in very different ways to respond to the particular internal and external constraints and pressures they face.

We start by looking at how ideas about organizing have spread to three particular unions: Unite, the GMB, and the Union of Shop, Distributive, and Allied Workers (USDAW). We have chosen these unions because they have been at the forefront of developing innovative ideas and practices, but also because they illustrate the diversity of organizing strategies that can be developed. These unions are also three of the largest in the United Kingdom. USDAW organizes in the retail and distribution sectors and has been a very active supporter of the TUC Organising Academy. Unite and the GMB are large, general unions organizing across a very wide range of sectors. They have been less directly involved in the TUC Academy than some unions (although the Transport and General Workers Union [TGWU] did sponsor two trainees), but they have been very involved with developing key parts of the training program, supporting the initiative within the TUC, and guiding TUC policy by sitting on the decision-making and oversight bodies that have responsibility for the New Unionism initiative and Organising Academy. It is therefore particularly interesting to see how organizing ideas have spread into these unions. In the second part of this chapter, we broaden our perspective to consider some wider questions about how organizing is managed and some of the tensions that can create. In this section we bring in reference to many other unions to highlight key issues.

Unite, the GMB, and USDAW have all taken on board organizing ideas by developing their own in-house training programs. These programs demand closer attention as they signal important developments in ideas about the purpose and practice of union organizing activity in the United Kingdom. Because these unions are large enough to develop tailored programs, it allows us to examine what they see organizing as being about and how they want to embed organizing practice within their specific contexts. First, we explain briefly what these programs entail, then consider their wider implications in relation to what the three unions seek to achieve through organizer training. All three unions have committed considerable resources to organizing. What we see is that they have taken very different approaches. The reasons for and consequences of those different approaches have profound implications for debates and discussions about how different unions understand the purpose of organizing, what they want the outcomes to be, and how they operationalize their plans. Throughout the book, we argue that we need to understand the complex social processes involved in union organizing. Many of these pressures exist outside of the union in the social, economic, political, and cultural contexts within which unions are operating. But a point that is often underdeveloped in many studies of union organizing is the extent to which union strategies are informed by internal constraints as well as external constraints. In other words, the politics and processes involved within the union are often equally important when we try to explain why organizing policies have emerged in the ways that they have.

Unite—TGWU: Specialization of the Organizing Role

Prior to its merger to form a new union called Unite in 2007, the TGWU had been experimenting with a number of innovative approaches to organizing activity. Unite (like the TGWU before it) is a large, general union organized across many sectors and representing around 1.2 million members[1]. Unite's organizing strategy rejected an approach that focused on organizing individual workplaces in favor of a more coordinated sectoral approach to seek to expand union recognition for bargaining rights into areas of the economy where unions have not historically been recognized. Initially, this involved focusing on a key sector and running campaigns in the largest employers with the intention of securing voluntary recognition for collective bargaining on the back of campaigns around workplace issues. If managers refused to concede a voluntary recognition agreement, the union would pursue a statutory agreement. The statutory procedures were always regarded as less favorable than voluntary recognition for a number of reasons. First, the range of issues over which the company is forced to negotiate is limited by law to pay, holidays, and working time. This was viewed by the union to be an almost unacceptably narrow range of issues and was therefore only seen as a starting point for expanding the scope of bargaining at a later stage. Second, the legal process is relatively lengthy and therefore costly. Finally, the explicit intention of the statutory recognition legislation was that it only be considered as a tactic of last resort.

Nonetheless, the existence of the statutory procedures from 1999 onward underpinned the union's sectoral strategy. By targeting large, influential employers within a particular sector, the union explicitly sought to take wages (and other terms and conditions) out of competition across a particular sector in a specific region. In other words, the disincentive for unionization would cease to be so influential if all employers in a sector recognized a union. Early applications of this strategy were visible in, for example, the casino sector, where the union limited its focus to the London labor market and was successful in gaining recognition agreements with

---

1. We have taken all membership figures from the official reports of the UK certification officer. We accept that measuring union membership accurately is difficult and participants have given us different figures at different times. The certification officer returns are taken as the official record of UK union membership, so those are the figures we quote here.

most of the large London casinos. On the back of such successes, the union could then approach smaller employers and attempt to develop a strategy of "pattern setting" in collective bargaining. A further strength of this approach is that within the union, these workers could be brought together within a sectoral and geographic branch structure. This could facilitate an exchange of information and solidarity across different employers and workplaces. Negotiating officers could also have the advantage of specialist knowledge about the specific labor market issues affecting a particular sector.

In an effort to "roll out" this strategy, and highly influenced by a strategic partnership with the Service Employees International Union (SEIU) in the United States, the TGWU began to invest heavily in sectoral organizing campaigns before the 2007 merger to form Unite. By 2008, the TGWU section of the new union employed nearly a hundred specialist organizers to target strategically important greenfield sectors. The union continues to be heavily committed to organizing activity since the merger. The initiative is led by two key national officers, one of whom is a graduate of the first year of the TUC Organising Academy. In interviews, they both explicitly acknowledge the influence of the TUC training program on their own strategy. One commented, "I pay tribute to what the TUC did because there is no doubt about it—the academy helped to put organizing on the map."

This quotation clearly shows the influence of the TUC Academy on the development of an organizing strategy in Unite. However, it is notable how different this sectoral strategy is from the idea of a "toolbox" of organizing practices that can be used to a variety of different ends. Here, Unite has been able to identify a clear *strategic objective*: taking wages out of competition across a regional sector. This objective has emerged from a realization of the potential weaknesses in seeking to organize individual workplaces, which would leave them open to wage competition from other employers in the sector, especially within a particular geographic region. The strategy of focusing on geographically and sectorally specific labor markets has been applied with some considerable degree of success in the white meat processing industry, in low-cost airlines, and to some degree in janitorial work in the business district of London (Wills 2008).

Central to the success of this strategy has been developing strong, independent networks of workplace activists who are trained and supported to take on a considerable degree of the bargaining and representation work. Activists are then brought together into what Unite calls Combine Committees. These committees are regionally based, often in the same city or town, and are made up of activists from different workplaces and different employers. The intention is that they share experience and help each other develop more effective workplace organization in a local area. The name of these committees is important. It is a deliberate echo of the strong workplace representation structures for which UK industrial relations was famous in the 1960s and 1970s. These committees are a deliberate effort to link workplace activists across sectors and put them at the heart of union's organizing strategy.

Within the officer corps, Unite has maintained the idea of organizing as a specialist activity, and as a consequence its training for organizers is more similar to the TUC's Academy than either the GMB or USDAW. In common with the TUC Organising Academy, Unite's organizers are relatively junior and specialize only in organizing work: negotiating and representation work is undertaken by other officers. However, because their efforts are focused sectorally, organizers have a relatively close relationship with generalist officers who take on bargaining and representation work. Generalist officers know when organizers are working on their "patch" and know that the outcome of successful recognition campaigns is likely to be the establishment of new branches, new agreements to be negotiated, and new representation to undertake. Although there is considerable variation in the extent to which individual officers embrace and engage with this work, there has been an effort to involve them in the organizing process. Importantly, generalist officers are also involved in organizing by developing activists in workplaces where recognition for bargaining is already established so that membership density in those workplaces increases. It is clear that this approach has the practical advantage of overcoming some of the difficulties that can arise if organizing work is managed separately from "servicing" work of negotiating and representation. But it is not the only way of managing this potential tension, and we see a very different approach in the GMB.

GMB—Mainstreaming Organizing Work

The GMB is a large, generalist union with just over 602,000 members in both the public and private sectors. Prior to the mid-2000s, in common with many other unions, there had been a formal and institutionalized separation of organizing and bargaining roles. Further, the GMB was well known for being a union that largely kept regions separate and independent from each other, described by several interviewees as a "balkanized" structure. Developments or initiatives in one of the nine regions rarely rolled out to others. In 2006 there was a change of senior leadership as Paul Kenny was elected as the general secretary. With this election came a marked change of approach to organizing. Kenny had previously been the regional secretary of the London region and had had significant success in developing an approach to organizing that had grown the regional membership by more than 20 percent in the preceding five years. This approach had focused on developing a small team of specialist organizers who planned strategic targeting of organizing resources. There was then a concerted effort to break down barriers between the work allocations of individual officers and activists to encourage an exchange of information between workplaces and campaigns. Unsurprisingly, one of the central objectives of the following years has been to roll out the approach to organizing that was developed in the early 2000s in the London Region while responding to the different labor markets and challenges being faced in other regions. To do this, the national union is working hard to facilitate an exchange of ideas and information between regions.

In sharp contrast to the Unite and TUC approaches, the GMB has taken the view that employing specialist organizers risks making organizing a separate activity within the union—something that "those organizers" do, rather than work that is integrated into the daily work of everyone who works for the union. In an effort to overcome this potential difficulty, the GMB decided to integrate organizing work into the roles of all officers. As explained by the national organizer, this was a decision that was taken in order to get the support of the officer corps for the organizing agenda:

> What is true is that the officer corps, because of the leadership of the union, are what needs to be shifted. All unions are dealing with this issue. How do you move your officer corps on in a humane, kindly way that gets them to buy in? ... So, my concern with the TUC is—with the OA [Organising Academy]—is ... that although you need, in the regions and nationally, small teams of specialist teams to make members—there is a real risk that if you go too far down that road—bringing in specialists—that you have the

opposite effect; you end up alienating them. You alienate the servicing and representing officers, either by them thinking "I don't need to recruit anyone, that's for specialists and they will do it," which is what we faced in the London region. If you are not careful you set up specialist organizing teams you will give the impression that officers no longer need to recruit. So, my concern with setting up an internal academy in the GMB would be that it would run counter to the message. The message could be "these specialists are going to come in and solve all the problems." (Martin Smith, national organizer, GMB)

This approach has the advantage of mainstreaming organizing activity as a core function of the union, but previous studies of the work of union officers (Kelly and Heery 1994) shows that the day-to-day pressures of representation and negotiating can tend to take over from the often more long-term responsibility of organizing work. The risk therefore is that organizing falls off the agenda in the face of the pressures of other commitments. In order to try to overcome this, the GMB has made it an essential requirement that all officers report on their organizing work and that this is a key part of objective setting and evaluation. Campaigns are reviewed every month, and emphasis is placed on getting "successful" regions to support their colleagues in regions where there have been more difficulties. There is also a strong view that officers should be involved in selecting the local targets and projects within the national plan, thus ensuring "ownership" of the projects at a local level.

We had to make sure that every region has a project board and on it will be the 3 national projects and no more than 6 regional projects. Your local projects should be picked using the same process, your officers, branches, etc. should pick these projects in the region through the same democratic processes—but how you do that is your own business but the same criteria should apply: access, issues, momentum. But we have not so far even called in reports on what these regional projects are—we have been hands off—let the democracy flourish! And, only if it isn't working... what I'm at pains to point out when we say it is bottom-up approach in terms of the principles we are pursuing, democracy is fundamental; it is not an add on at the end—it is central to success. (Martin Smith, national organizer, GMB)

This quotation directly addresses the issue of the challenges of balancing the central coordination of resources (specifically in the GMB case the selection of targets) while still maintaining the democratic principles of the union. This is a conceptually and practically interesting issue that we highlighted in chapter 2, and one we return to throughout the book. Others (Voss and Sherman 2000) have argued that organizing efforts are an example of where the "iron law of oligarchy" is conceptually problematic. The iron law of oligarchy (Michels 1915) suggests that political parties—and by extension labor unions—inevitably tend toward centralized control. Voss and Sherman (2000) argue that organizing and renewal activity in labor unions depends on activism at workplace level and therefore inevitably challenges efforts to centralize the process. These two are, they argue, in constant tension with each other. In the quotation above, we see an acceptance that these tensions are inherent within organizing initiatives and an attempt to reconcile them.

The GMB approach has been to use national level coordination to focus resources and efforts on strategically important targets, but then to allow local or regional officers to identify ways of implementing those plans. What is brought into particularly sharp focus in this case is the way that the very highest levels of the union are relying on a strategy that requires the involvement and support of the generalist officers. In trying to achieve this, the GMB has therefore focused on training generalist officers rather than specialist organizers. There are, nonetheless, four specialist organizers working for the union under the direct line management of the national organizer. Their role is to take a more strategic overview of the companies and workplaces being targeted for organizing and recruitment efforts. In interviews, they were keen to emphasize that this was largely informed by nationally set negotiating objectives. So, for example, if the union regarded school catering as a priority sector, the role of the organizers would be to develop a plan about how membership, activism, and structures can be built and strengthened in key geographical or employer areas. In addition, they train activists and promote a broader "organizing agenda" within the culture of the union. One of the four explained that:

> The first phase in terms of the three projects is about trying to remove that perception that there's iron curtains in the region. They've all gone now, and it's about people having the confidence to talk from one region to another about best practice.... We've done things in different regions where [there] have been some very positive results. But it's not been duplicated elsewhere.

It's now like people feel free to talk and that's what we're trying to do—adopt best practice. "Come forward and tell us what you did." ... It may not be perfect what took place in one region but if it's getting results then you can always tweak things if it moves along. ... And that's the role of the three projects [national targets]. Get people talking. It then follows through to start bringing ... the training, for the skills to develop, where they've got the self-ownership. (GMB organizer)

The importance of this centralized role was emphasized by the national organizer in our many, lengthy discussions and interviews. He had developed a particular approach to organizing during his career in the union movement; initially as a community organizer, then as the officer with responsibility for organizing within one of the regions of the GMB. He argued forcefully that the challenge of moving such a large union away from a culture that viewed membership as a function of providing good services meant that there was an important role for a degree of central allocation of resources. In other words, in order to overcome some of the deeply entrenched culture within the union, there had to be a degree of central oversight.

What we did do was to have a centralized control of those resources and what was interesting about the recruitment figures is that we were able to direct resources around the region to where people could get the best results and what that did was we overcame the rigid vertical hierarchical structure which previously had said this is the recruitment officer for Chelmsford office and they can't be used elsewhere. So we centralized resources so that we could direct people where we wanted them. (Martin Smith, national organizer, GMB)

He went on to give an important illustrative example of how this worked at a regional level:

A very good example was the Hackney office where they were adamant that they wanted to send their person around Hackney schools to recruit cleaners and that person did this for six months. During that time they managed to recruit eighteen to nineteen people, whereas three miles away another team was hitting schools and doing three to four meetings a day and were getting eight to ten members per day. They were crying out for another pair of hands to exploit this opportunity. But the insanity of the GMB structure at the time was that it was impossible to move one individual from one place to another. We gave ourselves in the London Region the way to solve that problem. The first month after we solved that problem we shifted our average growth to about 1,200–1,400 members per month and we stayed there. We were able to stop the nonsense of people guarding what little recruitment resource there was. (Martin Smith, national organizer, GMB)

Importantly, no one we spoke to in the union felt that the current culture was the "fault" of the officers. As one interviewee explained:

You can't blame the officers. By and large they have been recruited into a culture that has been drummed into them. A culture of getting Labour [Party] elected first, supporting the government blindly for whatever it would do for five to six years. So we have bought into anything they gave us; union learning, partnership, union modernization, and all that. And then someone made a sea change and said we now want you to do this [organizing] instead. (Martin Smith, national organizer, GMB)

This approach of engaging generalist officers and ensuring that organizing policy is delivered effectively has been taken forward and now forms the basis of the national initiatives. To this end, the union has developed a three-day organizing training program for all existing officers and a much more extensive training program for new officers. At the core of this training is the notion of "bargaining to organize" in other words to integrate bargaining and organizing work much more profoundly than could happen without integrating organizing into the work of generalist officers. The national organizer who has responsibility for developing this approach was actively involved in developing and delivering the TUC training program, and is very happy to recognize the influence of the TUC program on the current GMB strategy. But, he argues, the specific approach of the GMB has also been informed by the particular internal and external contexts within which the union operates. This approach stems from the analysis that throughout the late 1990s and early 2000s, the union expanded rapidly within key sectors and subsequently needed to consolidate its position. Increasing density in sectors such as catering services, cleaning services, and other contracted-out sectors will, it is hoped, increase bargaining leverage. National officers argue that without a sound organization in core sectors, bargaining leverage is at best seriously constrained, and at worst any bargaining gains secured can easily be undermined because implementation relies on management.

The integration of organizing work into the role of generalist officers is supported by the development of activists who specialize in organizing. Called workplace organizers, these are activists who work alongside officers to develop organizing plans for their own workplaces. Because of the large number of workplace representatives in a union the size of the GMB, one of the specialist organizers pointed out that "if you got 50 percent of those stewards [workplace representatives] thinking in a proactive way within a workplace, that's a radical change" (GMB organizer).

Under an agreement between the national union and the regions, this training program is run in the regions and is focused on how organizing tactics can develop and strengthen workplace representation structures. To the same end, the union has also established a biannual meeting for activists in order to exchange ideas and information. Together, the intention is to move away from the "traditional" view of training activists that typically conceptualizes training as an educational process in which information is given to participants and instruction prioritizes debate, discussion, and the sharing of ideas.

The approach in the GMB has been remarkably different from many unions and highlights an emerging theme of the potential for tension between specialist organizers and generalist officers. This is a theme we return to later and is an important issue underlying the development of organizing activity in UK unions. For the moment, however, we turn to examine a third, very different approach to managing organizing, that used by the retail and distribution union USDAW.

USDAW—Routinizing the Organizing Role

USDAW is a union representing just over 393,000 members mainly in the retail and distribution sectors. It was an early participant in the TUC Organising Academy and has sponsored as many as six organizers through the TUC program each year since 1998. USDAW was also well known for promoting a "partnership" approach to some of the large employers with which it has recognition and collective bargaining arrangements, particularly with Tesco, which is the UK's largest supermarket retailer. The union is faced with the challenge of having a membership turnover of around 30 percent per year, which is largely a function of the high labor turnover in the retail sector, and which has important implications for membership and organizing. Even though it is common for workers to move within the sector, there are large sections of retail that are nonunionized.

In contrast to many academic commentators (Carter and Fairbrother 1998, Kelly 1999), USDAW sees no inherent conflict between organizing and a partnership. To them, a constructive relationship with the employer is desirable as it allows access to the workplace, which facilitates recruitment and organizing activity. The union uses these relationships with key large employers to secure agreements that allow them to talk to all new hires at their induction. Inductions typically take place weekly in large retail employers and often as many as fifteen new hires may be present. A union recruiter (usually an official, an organizer, or an activist) will be allowed a period of time at the end of the meeting to make a short presentation about the union and to get as many new recruits as possible to join. Skilled recruiters have an incredibly high success rate and regularly spoke to us about being able to recruit more than 90 percent of any such audience. Learning how to recruit in this way is a core skill for all USDAW officers and organizers, and they have developed an in-house training program to promote this approach. As one national union official explained:

> If we could get ourselves a 100 percent membership in Tesco's, Sainsbury's, Morrison's and the Co-op [supermarket chains] then we would effectively double the size of our union. So we wanted to give our academy an USDAW spin which was around, not greenfield recruitment, but a very, very high turnover. We lose 80,000 members a year. So some of the very slow burn organizing models that the TUC Academy put forward wouldn't necessarily work in an USDAW environment. So we wanted to give it our spin in terms of being able to recruit and organize in a retail environment. (Carl Parker, training officer USDAW)

Within this context, USDAW has developed a unique approach to organizing training. The union has developed a six-month training program—which they call their Organising Academy—that is targeted at workplace activists. Typically coming from one of the large retailers with whom

USDAW has good recognition rights, these activists are given leave from their usual job in order to participate in the program. The union pays their employers the equivalent of their wages and the employee is released to work for the union for the six months of the program with the expectation that they return to their job at the end of the training. During the six months, the union trains them to go into workplaces with a focus on recruiting members, identifying activists, and identifying issues that are relevant to that workforce. In common with the other unions, the training is highly influenced by the TUC program, but is narrower, is specific to the kinds of workplaces within which USDAW is recognized, and is assessed with fewer written assignments.

One of the lead trainers explained in detail the way the training is designed to build the skills and understanding necessary for workplace organizing:

> This is where it's different from the TUC Academy, I think. But there are five training courses within the six month program; more at the front, fewer towards the end of the program. And we try and build from a position where people start. So we start by developing one-to-one recruitment skills. There is a lot of padding around the organizing model and what we mean by the organizing model. Which is entirely TUC-led. You know, the whole sort of organizing side, organizing around issues, all of that is there. But we start with one-to-one recruitment. And sending people away for three weeks to go and recruit in small workplaces where we know it's relatively easy to recruit. So not where you are going to be hit by big organization barriers or institutional barriers to recruit.... So it's really just a confidence-building exercise but also honing one-to-one skills. We then go on to sort of recruiting in larger environments such as inductions. But still at the same time on the training, building their understanding of organizing. So then people go away and do that for two or three weeks. Then we start to, then we start to ask people to be running minicampaigns. So they will be going away and running in a couple of larger workplaces.... They would be planning, they'd be, absolutely everything would be their responsibility. So early on we are introducing the concept of mapping and things like that. And then one of their projects will be go away and map a workplace. So by round about week eight we are asking people to go to—with the intention of them talking to reps rather than doing it themselves by this point—to start to work with reps in the workplaces, to identify new reps, to map the store, getting a profile of the store, and to start running a short

campaign, a four-week campaign, issue-based, and we normally pick on one of the national campaigns for the issue so like parents and carers campaign, Freedom From Fear campaign. Let them run the campaign there and really as a precursor for the final three months. For people to be given four or five workplaces for them to organize those four or five workplaces. (Carl Parker, training officer USDAW)

A central rationale for the establishment of the union-specific program was the fact that USDAW wanted far more people to be trained as organizers than could have feasibly gone through the TUC program. As a key decision maker pointed out, there were a number of reasons why this was deemed to be unfeasible:

I think we've known that the TUC Academy long-term couldn't be fully sustainable for us in terms of training. Training sufficient numbers of people.... Because if you put someone to the TUC Academy I think there is always an assumption that there will be an expectation that they carried on in employment [in a union]. Now you can't take three or four people on every year and continue to employ because you just grow the full-time officer base too much.... And I think we were also at a stage where we wanted to be able to do something that we could take our very best reps and offer them something more. Because there's always been a frustration that you can train people to a level and then it kind of dries up.... And maybe the final thing was that we also knew that the TUC Academy had a fairly heavy emphasis on greenfield organizing, which for USDAW was never and probably never will be, our priority. (Carl Parker, training officer USDAW)

Within this approach, organizing activity is seen as relatively routinized work. In other words, there are particular tactics and arguments that are routinely used to encourage members to join. Unsurprisingly within this context, there is a strong emphasis on recruiting large numbers of members, but the organizers are always keen to try to identify potential activists. Again, they have a series of arguments ready to counter any objections and keep lists of people that they think might be appropriate as activists but who, for whatever reasons, cannot take on the role immediately. Target workplaces are selected to ensure that they get regular visits from either officers or organizers and the information about membership, activists, and issues are managed within a large database. Given some of the criticisms of the TUC training discussed in the previous chapter, it is important to note that organizers have very little input into the strategic decision making. Indeed, the strategic roles discussed previously (selecting targets, seeing through a campaign from beginning to end, and linking organizing to bargaining) are largely left to generalist officers, with organizers doing the bulk of the routine work of recruiting members and identifying potential activists.

This approach is clearly informed by the need to keep recruiting members to account for the heavy losses that such a high turnover in retail inevitably brings. But it crucially relies on access being granted by the employer. It is therefore underpinned by USDAW's famous "partnership" approach, which seeks to secure employer support for unionization. The agreement at Tesco supermarket chain is the most well-known example and that agreement gives the union rights to attend all briefings of new employees, for officers and organizers to access the workplace whenever they want, and to actively encourage workers to join the union. In exchange, the employer secures the cooperation of the union, for example, in restructuring efforts, or in other culture change programs. Although Tesco is probably the most developed and well-established initiative of this kind, the union seeks similar agreements with other employers where possible. At minimum, it seeks to secure good workplace access in order to undertake the kind of organizing activity described above.

The union argues forcefully that this is a clear example of how partnership and organizing can sit alongside each other. Senior officials also emphasize that this strategy is informed by the inability of the union to rely on militancy among its membership. They argue that the nature of retail employment means that a moderate approach is both necessary and desirable for its members. Indeed it was partly the particular constraints faced within the labor market that inspired the union to develop its approach. There was a strong view within the union that the TUC Organising Academy placed too great an emphasis on organizing in greenfield sites to secure recognition and that there had to be quite a degree of adaptation to translate that approach to the kind of recruitment and organizing context faced by USDAW. This was not an uncommon view among many sponsoring unions in the early stage, and much work has been done both by the TUC and by sponsoring unions to work out how to adapt and apply organizing ideas within the specific contexts they face.

What Explains the Variation in the Spread of Organizing Ideas and Practice?

What these three examples show is how influential the TUC training has been on the development of organizing training in individual unions, even where those unions have not participated in the academy by directly sponsoring trainees. And we see the importance of two key factors in shaping organizing strategy and practice in these unions: external influences relating to the particular groups of workers and labor markets within which the union operates, and internal influences such as the history, politics, and structure of the union.

We can see in all of the three unions that have adopted their own organizing training that the labor market conditions in which they organize are, unsurprisingly, a central influence on the particular form and approach that they have taken. The clearest example is USDAW, which focuses so tightly on recruiting large numbers of members because of the very high labor turnover rates in the labor market in which they organize. This informs a particular approach to organizing activity and focuses efforts toward developing efficient and effective systems that secure fast membership gains. Within this context, it is entirely rational to systematize and routinize the recruitment process. Organizing activity then becomes focused on identifying and training workplace activists. Also the influence of the labor market on the role of activists is clear. The low-skill nature of much of the work in the retail and distribution sector means that these workers often have comparatively low levels of basic literacy and numeracy skills. Structuring activist training around tried and tested ways to recruit and organize helps to develop their skills, confidence, and experience, which is essential if they are to challenge managers.

Another example of the ways the external labor market in which the union operates has influenced organizing strategy is in Unite. Focused on greenfield expansion into previously unorganized areas of the economy, the union has faced a considerable degree of resistance and hostility from employers. To counter this, the union needs a pool of expert resources that can be intensively targeted against individual employers at key moments in a campaign. Having a group of skilled and experienced specialist organizers is therefore extremely useful in this kind of campaign.

Although external influences are important in explaining how and why specific organizing strategies are developed in particular unions, it is also important that we recognize the role of internal factors such as the policies, history, and politics within unions. A particularly clear example of this is the emphasis that Unite places on the committees bringing together workplace representatives. This is a deliberate attempt to reinvent and revitalize the principle of strong shop stewards (workplace representatives) for which the TGWU (often shortened to the T&G) has been well known. As one interviewee put it:

> Now we learn from our own history. It's not new and it's not rocket science. What we are doing is rooted in our own history, we are rebuilding that strong self-confident, self-sustaining workplace organization, led by effective shop stewards. That was at the heart of T&G when it was 2 million strong and it's important to stress that—and it would be a mistake to deny that history. We should be proud and actually it can help to dictate what you're doing in the context of your history. (TGWU assistant general secretary)

Another example of how the particular history and politics of a union influences the adoption of organizing ideas can be seen in USDAW's commitment to partnership arrangements with Tesco, which creates the context for the kind of leave arrangements necessary for much of their organizing activity. Similarly, the GMB strategy to roll out some national organizing targets and tactics has been driven, at least in part, by an effort to try to coordinate regional organizing activity, which is a policy response to a particular history and structure of that union. In addition to the external influences of labor markets and employer behavior, these internal historical, political, and structural factors help explain how and why organizing looks so different in different contexts. Nonetheless, what we see across different unions are similar strategic questions and issues arising, particularly in relation to the two themes discussed in the opening chapters: how to build union power and how to engage democratic structures. We have seen how, in practice, these two broad questions relate to two much more specific tensions visible in organizing activity: first, how to balance organizing activity with the pressure to provide effective services to members, and second, how to deploy the specialist skills of organizers.

How Is Organizing Managed in Other Unions?

As we have already shown, one of the central features of the TUC's organizing training from the mid-1990s onward was a growing belief that organizing activity needed to become a *specialist function* within UK unions. We see from the examples of the three unions we have just discussed that different unions have in fact operationalized organizing strategies in different ways with some, like the GMB, arguing for a more integrated approach while others, like Unite, see a clear advantage in specialization. In this section, we want to consider the tensions and issues raised by the ways in which organizers are managed within unions and, in particular, focus on the challenges and tensions that can emerge between specialist organizers and generalist officers, because this reveals a great deal about the internal challenges to developing and implementing effective organizing strategies.

The emphasis on managing organizing as a separate, specialist function emerged in part from the realization that declining resources made it difficult for generalist officers to have time to engage in expansionist recruitment and organizing activity, and also from recognition that the day-to-day responsibilities of representation and negotiation often took priority over the longer term—and risky—organizing roles (Kelly and Heery 1994). In the early stages of thinking through what organizing meant in the UK context, a rather artificial differentiation was drawn between "organizing" and "servicing" roles. This approach conceived of the organizing role as a largely separate function within the union that was solely engaged with building and developing membership. Core activities included recruitment, identifying representatives and activists, mapping workplaces to identify areas where membership was (potentially) strong or weak, and identifying grievances that might be the basis of collective action. Explicitly excluded from organizing roles was any individual representation, collective bargaining, or negotiation, as these were seen to be the function of the generalist officers.

However, it quickly became apparent that while the differentiation between "servicing" and "organizing" functions may have been conceptually helpful in explaining the envisaged "new" role of organizers, it was not always a practical differentiation in day-to-day activity. Indeed it set up a division, which in practice, was not always possible (nor desirable) to sustain. In practice, the development of a specialist organizing function brings with it profound challenges in managing organizers. For example, how are organizers used within the structure of the union? How do they fit in with other union activity, especially those of generalist officers? And how do they cope with the tensions and challenges that their specialist function brings? These questions fundamentally relate to the debate about whether organizers should be deployed mainly to *recruit* new members, or whether they should undertake a wider role by, for example, developing new representational structures, organizing in workplaces that did not have recognition, and the like. A central part of the rhetoric of organizing training and practice is that it is important not to *solely* focus on membership numbers but also to concentrate on the effectiveness and sustainability of building membership and developing member self-organization. Interesting questions therefore emerge about the extent to which some unions have been using trained organizers for simple recruitment activities, rather than building more sustainable membership structures.

Unsurprisingly, there is considerable variation between unions and between experienced and less-experienced organizers. Our research tends to suggest, however, that organizers are often an underused resource. For example, we surveyed organizers at the end of their training year at the TUC Organising Academy. The vast majority of them (more than 70 percent) had been regularly involved in the more routine aspects of organizing activity such as face-to-face recruitment, leafleting, and other activities intended to raise the profile of the union. This is not particularly surprising; these roles are central to organizing work, and there is often a view that organizers need to "cut their teeth" by engaging in these routine aspects of organizing work. Much more surprising was the fact that only just over half of organizers said they frequently identified grievances as the basis for organizing. Similar numbers reported that they regularly mapped workplaces in order to establish whether or not workers were likely to join a union, and established workplace organizing committees. This lends further weight to the argument we started to make in previous chapters that organizers' skills tend to be used in a more ad hoc rather than strategic manner, particularly at the start of their careers.

Two possible explanations for these findings present themselves. First, it is possible that in junior traineeship roles, organizers are being deployed primarily to do recruitment work with the intention that they then build their skills to focus on broader organizing efforts. Second, it is possible that unions are failing to use and engage the full range of skills of specialist organizers. Our research indicates that it seems probable that both explanations have some merit. Even in the three unions we have profiled above (GMB, Unite, and USDAW) where there is a clear organizing strategy, it is rare that organizers themselves develop these strategies or even develop campaign-level strategies because, as we shall see later, very few trained organizers have any opportunity for career progression to senior levels of the specialist role. What has emerged strongly from our recent research is that many organizing roles remain low-status and at a very junior level. In the following chapter, we discuss the effects of this on the career progression of individual organizers. Here we want to focus on the consequences of this for the management of organizing in individual unions and how this can create and perpetuate tensions between specialist organizers and generalist officers.

Status of Organizers

The status of organizers—and by implication organizing—within their unions is of profound concern to many of our interviewees. Organizers and other senior union officials routinely told us that there is a strong perception (and in many cases reality) within British unions that organizing is a junior, entry-level position. As one organizer told us, "I think some people don't respect the organizing role. They see it as an easy role. [That] it's not as intensive as a full-time official role, with casework and things like that to do. But I actually think it's the other way around" (OA organizer #91, black male). Another Organising Academy graduate told us how this status difference was reinforced by a job evaluation exercise: "Also there's been a job evaluation exercise which has graded the organizing role as lesser than a negotiating role. And I think that, to some extent, it is an indicator of the sort of wider problem" (OA organizer #127, white female). In many unions, organizing work is also usually paid less than that of other generalist union officials.

> What you should do, pay the organizers the same as the officers, that would sort it almost overnight. Because we live in the society where status,

however unfair that might be, status is—generally within an organization—determined by your salary. And if you're paid six grand [six thousand pounds] more than somebody else, the perception within that organization will be that you're senior. And you can't change that just by saying "Oh we're all the same." (OA organizer #45, white male)

Further, although there is a common perception that organizing is an entry-level role, many get "stuck" at this junior level. One senior policymaker within the TUC commented that this was potentially a serious problem.

There are issues about progression. We've got lots of good organizers who came through year 1, year 2, year 3 and some of them are still doing exactly the same jobs that they came into the movement sort of 9, 10 years ago now. It's not to say that it's not important that they're organizing, but I think there's actually a lot of good people—a lot of good women, in particular—organizers who are stuck in organizing roles and who can't progress because the unions just don't have any real progression route for them. (Union official #20, white male)

Almost all interviewees reported that pay was typically considerably lower than for officer grades they viewed as being equivalent and this was a reason why organizers (often reluctantly) moved on to other roles within the union when they could. One academy graduate who was now working as a generalist officer commented that this move had caused some concern within his work group, but deliberately attributed his desire to make this move as being motivated by the desire for progression within the union movement: "I think partially the reason for, they've been disquiet about me moving across was that it's seen as a progression rather than as a sideways move if you like. But again, there was no career structure with organizing" (OA organizer #43, white male). Another commented that "you can't progress your way up the union [by being an organizer]. OK some people have, but most people, the most likely way to progress up the union is through being a full time official, or regional officer of the union" (OA organizer #91, black male). Linking together all of these themes, another graduate pointed out that the status, pay, and progression issues were all important in why organizing roles were often seen as entry-level positions: "If you have the organizers paid less than officers, you have automatically got a problem. Because one of two things happen. Either they use it as a stepping stone to become an officer and we lose all our very good organizers out to the officer corps. Or it becomes a training ground for other unions" (OA organizer, #24 white male).

There are many more comments along similar lines emerging from the interview data. Importantly, they are not limited to those who trained a long time ago, and these views are shared by both those who currently work as specialist organizers and by those who have moved into more generalist roles. But these are not the only indications that the union movement as a whole may not be using the resources provided by these skilled organizers in the most effective manner.

In the 2007 survey of Organising Academy graduates, 39 percent of respondents with a specialist organizing role reported that they would, ideally, like to use their organizing skills more. This is further evidence that a significant minority of organizers feel that they are stuck in relatively junior positions where they do not feel they have sufficient scope to use the range of skills for which their training equipped them. Together with the interview data we can see that a significant minority of graduates are frustrated with the way in which their employing union understands and applies ideas about organizing. Specifically, organizing approaches that focus more on quantitative recruitment targets rather than building membership structures appear to be a source of frustration for most organizers. Organizers generally remain positive about the opportunities for their unions to change and develop, but the sense of fighting an entrenched culture is palpable and they often see their ability to promote cultural change as constrained by their junior status.

When they did receive a perceived "promotion" to a generalist office role, although organizing was no longer their main activity, trained organizers typically reported that they tried to incorporate organizing practice into their work and tried to use what they had learned to encourage lay activists to develop an organizing approach in their branches. This is an interesting development as it emphasizes the need to try to change the culture of unions at all levels, from lay activists to senior management, but it is also important to note that many felt that they had greater opportunity to promote cultural change as officers than as organizers because they were more deeply integrated into the core activities of the union. This issue takes us to the ways in which relationships between organizers and generalist officers are managed within different unions. The testimonies of organizers, generalist officers, and senior officials all emphasize the fact that there are profound tensions between the roles of specialist organizers and generalist officers that are often not captured in a simplistic analysis of organizing work in which organizing is seen as being in opposition to servicing work.

Relationships between Officers and Organizers

As we have seen, there is considerable scope for unions to manage and structure the organizing function in different ways and with different objectives. What is conceptually important is that even though unions have adopted different approaches, appropriate structures for managing relationships between organizers and officers remains a core debate within unions. The extent to which organizing can or should be a separate, specialist function within unions is an issue discussed throughout our research. Sound arguments have been put forward for diametrically opposing views, demonstrating that context and individual circumstances within different unions are central in determining the extent to which organizing is regarded as the role of specialist organizers or integrated into the work of all officers. These decisions clearly affect the relationships between the two groups as they deal with the policy and power structures within their unions.

There was considerable evidence from both generalists and specialists verifying the perception that generalist officers often got caught up in "firefighting" with little time for longer-term and more strategic activity. An example that was often given was the pressure of having a member on the telephone with a problem that had to be dealt with quickly, or a sudden announcement of redundancy affecting a large group of union members. Previous research (Kelly and Heery 1994) shows clearly how these pressures then force less immediately urgent issues down the "to do" list, meaning that organizing activity is often lowest on the list. One officer emphasized that unless organizing was made a routine part of his working day—which it is not currently—then firefighting would always take priority: "We're firefighting, that's the same point all the time—as an officer you're firefighting every day. And therefore you move with that concept of organizing being a routine" (Generalist officer #19, white male). From an organizer's perspective, this can present challenges in securing the support of generalist officers: "When I speak to officials now who are new...they still say that they don't have the time to organize....Once a pack of redundancies come in, everything else is dropped. Once the tribunal comes in, everything else is dropped and there's no time for the other things" (OA organizer #104, white female).

Securing the support of generalist officers for the work of organizers was a central concern to interviewees. The option to have a cadre of specialists who are largely removed from the representation and negotiation work done by generalist officers is an approach to organizing that is heavily influenced by some of the large US unions, most notably the SEIU. Right from the outset, many key decision makers have argued that organizing work demands specialist skills and resources that are not available within the existing, generalist officer corps. Within Unite, for example, decision makers commented that it would be extremely difficult to run the kind of intensive and cross-employer campaign such as Justice for Cleaners if they did not employ a large group of specialist organizers: "In terms of the launch of major organizing campaigns it would be inconceivable, to be frank, that we could mount the campaigns we are doing now using the existing officer corps" (Generalist officer #5, white male). Although this view partly reflected the view that officers would probably not have sufficient time to engage with the kind of aggressive, grassroots organizing activity of, for example, the Justice for Cleaners campaign, it also reflected a view that such activity demands specialist, and often strategic, skills and knowledge.

> I think certainly when it comes to greenfield work, you need people to very much focus on how strategically to take things forward. And that's a full time job and certainly my experience as a branch secretary is that organizing can come way down on the list of priorities when you have other responsibilities and folk are crying out for immediate attention on different things. (OA organizer #28, white male)

However, a potential weakness of this approach is that generalist officers may become too reliant on a specialist organizing team to do this work. This presents the possibility either that they may choose to disengage from organizing activities, or that they do not have sufficient training and experience to understand how the two roles link together. A commonly expressed opinion about organizing being an entirely separate function within unions is that creating such a division can undermine the hard work of the officer corps. One trained organizer commented:

> "[There are] big problems about just…bringing in a whole new layer of people who are doing a different job to the existing full time officer corps and put[ting] them together and expecting things to run smoothly. And a lot of…existing full time officers saying this is a real challenge. [They say] 'What I've been doing for the last 15–20 years? You tell me what I'm doing is not valuable any more?" (OA organizer #26, white male)

This was seen as a much wider problem with the way the TUC Organising Academy was initially promoted. The organizers were held up as being the "future of the trade union movement" and in one speech senior officers at the TUC acknowledged that this had been something of a "hostage to fortune" because it undermined much of the good work of generalist officers. It had the effect of building barriers between the two groups of professionals and entrenching resistance to organizing activity that has only started to be overcome much more recently. Some unions are gradually moving toward an approach that encourages generalists and specialists to work closely together in an effort to overcome some of these barriers. One organizer in a large union reported that she worked closely with the generalist officers in her area and that this gave a profound advantage both to her daily working life, but also to members:

> They [officers] are the ones who everybody is familiar with. They are the ones who the reps trust, the conveners trust. And it's by showing that solidarity I think within that workplace that the organizer, the officer, the convener and the reps and it builds like a family group to me. Whereas if you are just going to leave out the officer—who is the most important person as the members see it because at the end of the day that's the person who is going to be negotiating their terms and conditions and their wages and they see that person as someone like being important—and then when they see these outside people coming in trying to boost up the numbers, they see them as just an external resource. Just there to look good and to build up the numbers and then bugger off again. They don't see them as permanent fixtures. Whereas the officer is the person who they see quite constantly. And it kind of gives you two sides to the union. (OA organizer #87, black female)

But crucially, she went on to conclude that "there is no togetherness, I don't think, not at all." The view that organizers and generalist officers should work closely together was not particularly widely held but was well-argued by those who held it. Another academy graduate who now works as a generalist officer in a small union saw the size of her union as a central reason why specialists and generalists were forced, by circumstance, to work more closely together: "I think because we are so small that, you know, actually we have to work together. There is not a lot of room in this organization for two groups of employees to clash" (OA organizer #96, white female). She also emphasized that because the two groups worked closely together they were more effective and there were fewer tensions. She went on to give the following example:

> I work very closely with the organizers that are ... on the patches that I deal with. So we can come to that kind of accommodation but that really does involve very regular communications. It also involves organizers actually really understanding what is going on in the negotiation process. Which very often they don't. But also they can't because they are so busy doing their own role that they don't really have the time to understand the detail of what's going on. I mean, you know, I was speaking to one of the organizers that works on one of the patches I negotiate for ... and there was a massive negotiating issue that kicked off on that patch recently and I was, I was saying, "You know, it would be really useful if we could do a nonmembers newsletter" because it was actually a major headache. [laughs] And a massive issue that affected the terms for our members and we turned it into a mass event. And I said, "You know, that's such a big achievement we actually need to be using that. Both to tell our members, remind our members why we are here, the ones that weren't affected, but also to nonmembers. This is an advantage, this is the type of thing we can do." (OA organizer #96, white female)

So far, we have only considered the ways in which specialist organizers might be integrated into the work of the unions. However, there is also a further trend that demands consideration. Several large unions, including the GMB and the Public and Commercial Services Union (PCS), are developing integrated roles that seek to combine organizing and negotiating/servicing work into the roles of all officers. As we have seen in the previous section, this view has been clearly developed by the GMB. But the GMB is not the only union developing this approach. Some PCS interviewees also expressed concern that the development of specialist organizers might lead to organizing being seen as not part of the core role of generalist officers.

However, some organizers expressed profound apprehension about the integration of organizing into the generalist officer role. Reflecting the concerns about firefighting in the generalist role, one organizer in a different union explained:

> [There is] a move towards something called an industrial officer which is supposed to be something which incorporates both an organizing and a negotiating bargaining role, which I think as a model of something to move towards is probably quite good because it's about integrating organizing into the main role of the union. But I think the problem at the moment is that many of those people that are currently negotiating don't really understand organizing or are not committed to it. And what is likely if you merge the roles at the moment is that you'll lose much of the organizing focus and probably will be overcome by personal cases and bargaining and so forth. (OA organizer #27, white male)

This specialist organizer clearly saw this approach as undermining the professionalization and specialization of the organizing function. However, others were much more supportive of this "mainstreaming" approach: "I think that's the way [my union] prefers it. Well certainly has done for the fairly sort of long-term past. Has been to have both—people doing both roles, recruiting and organizing and their representing and whatever. And if I'm being honest I think that is right. I think that, particularly for smaller unions, that's the way it should be" (OA organizer #39, white male). Interestingly, one officer who was an academy graduate, but who now undertakes a considerable amount of casework, noted that one of the factors that made it particularly difficult to integrate organizing work into his role was the proliferation of casework. He attributed this to the increasing complexity of UK labor law, which has, over the past ten years or so, granted increasing numbers of individual rights to workers on issues such as discrimination, parental leave, a national minimum wage, maximum working hours, and paid holiday entitlement.

> There is a major proliferation of casework. Most, a lot of it, I've got seven at the moment, disability cases, which are really complex. And so you have law, as employment law becomes much more diverse and intertwined with

religious belief, disability, gender it can become extremely complicated. So
that takes up a hell of a lot of time. And that really cuts into your organizing time. (OA organizer #24, white male).

In practice, though, specialist organizers certainly recognized the important roles of negotiation and representation. What they questioned was
how that was integrated and the extent to which generalist officers also accepted the need for the organizing role. Where unions had chosen to keep
the organizing role as a separate specialist activity, almost without exception, organizers and senior officers were aware of the necessity of engaging generalist officers, at very least because any effort to change the culture
of the union requires their input. As one of our interviewees succinctly put
it: "With full time officials they have to be involved in the process [of orga-
nizing] because if they're not involved in the process one way or another,
if they're not working alongside an organizer say, on a particular project,
then it's going to fall down" (OA organizer #39, white male).

Conclusions

In this chapter, we have looked at how the efforts of the TUC to promote
organizing activity since the mid-1990s have spread into different unions.
The dominant assumption has been to manage organizing as a separate,
specialist activity. Where that has happened, organizers have often faced
the challenge of trying to promote cultural change and a shift of emphasis of
activity within the union while being in relatively junior positions. This
has been a source of tension with generalist officers. In an effort to address
this problem, some unions have attempted to mainstream the organizing
role into the activities of all union professionals. In these unions—most notably the GMB and PCS—there is still a role for specialist organizers, but
they work much more closely and directly with generalist officers. Here, of
course, the danger is that organizing slips off the agenda when faced with
workplace problems that require fast responses.

The important issue is that these different ways of structuring the roles
of officers and organizers have considerable implications for the relationships and tensions that emerge. In unions that have large groups of specialist organizers, there is a tendency for organizing to be seen as a very

separate function and for generalist officers to be brought into campaigns as a support or for their own development and training. In unions that attempt to facilitate officers and organizers working alongside each other, an effort is made to integrate and link the two roles more effectively, but success in achieving that objective often depends on the personal working relationships of those involved. There can be many advantages to this arrangement, but if officers or organizers are unable or unwilling to engage in the process, it can cause considerable tension. The third option is for unions to develop generalist roles, which includes organizing activity as a central part of the job description. There are far fewer examples of this approach, but as we have seen, the main disadvantage is the risk that organizing activity falls down the list of priorities.

It is probably unsurprising that the dominant view of organizers is that there is a necessity for organizing to continue to develop as a specialist role. This seems to result from a clear sense of professional unity and the view that outside of the organizing departments, many other union officials either do not fully understand or have not bought into the need for a fundamental shift to a new organizing culture. There is, however, a growing recognition that the divide between "organizing" work and "servicing" work is unhelpful in practical terms and an impediment to changing the broader culture of unions. Although the distinction between "organizing" and "servicing" was extremely helpful in the early days in explaining what the Organising Academy was seeking to achieve and how it was different to what unions had been doing for many years, it has led to a number of very profound challenges. First, there is a real danger of simplifying organizing into one, homogeneous set of practices that can be applied in an acontextual and ahistorical manner. Second, there is also the danger that because there is a lack of consensus about exactly what an "organizing union" looks like, there is scope for such a wide range of activities to be interpreted as organizing work that the term becomes meaningless. Finally, it may be interpreted in a way that suggests that there is no role for bargaining and representation work by paid union professionals—or that this is a peripheral activity and that it is "old unionism."

We argue that while there are practical differences between organizing activities and servicing work, any union must structure itself so that both are achieved effectively. What we see in UK unions is a range of different efforts to manage those activities. We also see that different contexts lead to different outcomes and tensions. In seeking to explain how and why unions adopt particular structures to manage organizing, we can clearly identify internal and external pressures. These include the labor market within which the union operates and, related to this, the kinds of workers being organized, as well as internal pressures and constraints such as the history, politics, and structure of the union. These different ways of managing organizing also have profound effects on organizers themselves, and it is to their stories and voices that we now turn.

4

UNION ORGANIZERS AND THEIR STORIES

Right from the outset of the Organising Academy, it was clear that the main role of the new organizers was to be "agents of change" within unions. We have been at pains to point out that, of course, organizing activities were taking place in UK unions prior to the mid-1990s. What changed with the development of the academy was a clear view that these new and relatively junior recruits would provoke a debate about the practice and importance of organizing activity within unions. Underpinning those ideas was the intention that the central objective of the process of change would be a more expansionist, inclusive, and participatory form of trade unionism. But at the outset there was little evidence of a comprehensive or overarching strategy to achieve these objectives in either individual unions, or across the labor movement more widely, and as we have seen in the previous chapter, there are many ways in which those ideas spread into individual unions. Consequently, over the past decade the role of organizer has developed largely in an ad hoc manner. We believe that it is important to examine the role of organizer in different unions and the challenges faced by those who have taken on this demanding and important position.

Organizing training in all of the unions and at the TUC Academy is an intense and challenging experience for participants, and it is designed to equip graduates with the skills not just to become organizers but to promote a particular approach to trade unionism that emphasizes membership participation and activism. Yet, as we have already identified, this can bring organizers into conflict with others within their own unions, and it raises questions about how union organizing work should be understood and managed. For example, where does the responsibility of an organizer start and finish? What role do organizers play in relation to other union officers? How do these new recruits manage the tensions within their role, and what consequences does this have on their lives outside work? Why is organizing largely perceived as a junior role, and what does this say about union commitment to the organizing agenda?

The aim of this chapter is to explore and explain the work that organizers do and the difficulties they face in affecting change. Clearly, not all union organizers have been trained through the TUC's Organising Academy, but a great many of them have, and we estimate that more than half, and probably nearer to two-thirds, of the UK union organizer workforce (around three hundred employees) have graduated from the TUC Organising Academy. We want to look at what they do in their roles before considering wider issues about the role of specialist organizers in relation to generalist officers and the tensions that are sometimes caused in these relationships.

In contrast to the United States (Milkman and Voss 2004a, Rooks 2004, Foerster 2003) very few studies of union organizing in the United Kingdom have focused directly on the experiences of organizers, and we know comparatively little about organizers' lives, their work experiences, and their career progression. Although there is some work on gender and diversity in the context of union democracy (Colgan and Ledwith 2002a, 2002b) and the impact of race and gender on the role of union activists (Healy et al. 2004a, Holgate 2004b), there is little known about how these factors affect the daily lives of organizers as *employees*. Understanding the working lives of organizers is essential if we are to understand the complex process of union renewal efforts taking place in UK unions. While there have been studies of "traditional" union officials or "full-time officers" (Kelly and Heery 1989, 1994), the role of specialist union organizer is relatively new, and as such there has been little opportunity to develop an understanding of the nature and influence of the position within unions.

The intention of this chapter is therefore to explore what it is like to work as a specialist organizer, the impact the role has had on changing union culture toward a more strategic type of organizing, and the impact the role has on the careers and personal lives of those undertaking this work.

Motivation to Train as a Union Organizer

The main motivating factors for the decision to train as a union organizer were broadly similar for the majority of academy graduates: they wanted to contribute to changing the union movement and assisting workers to assert their rights. In short, they wanted to "make a difference" in the way people are treated at work. Many saw the role of organizer more as a vocation rather than a job and spoke almost evangelically about union organizing:

> [I wanted] to be involved in inspiring others to become involved in active, campaigning trade union activities; transforming attitudes and lives; fighting employers and leading the way for better employment rights, and greater representation and involvement of disenfranchised workers and communities. (OA organizer #127, white female)

There was, it was believed, a necessity to transform the union movement so that it was truly capable of representing and defending vulnerable workers. As expressed by one organizer, "It's kind of our duty as trade unionists to have a collective response to ensure that vulnerable people are ok, and more than ok actually" (OA organizer #63, white female).

As might be expected given that most had experience of the union movement, organizers were acutely aware of the difficulties that unions had experienced over the preceding decades, but they were more than just aware—they had given considerable thought to how the union movement needed to change. No doubt the process of undertaking a year-long training program with a small cohort of other organizers, where people came together throughout that year for residential training, meant that there was plenty of time for discussion and debate about previous experiences and the future of the union movement. This meant that organizers were able to develop an overall view of different union strategies and approaches to organizing in a way that many others in the union movement were unable to do from the limited perspective of their own unions. Academy trainees were in a relatively unusual position; they had an overall perspective of organizing potential and activity because their training explicitly requires them to share experiences with organizers from other unions informed by their experiences in different workplaces and sectors. In some sense, the ability to see the "big picture" was one that was perceived not to be fully shared by others within their unions—not because other union officers were incapable of such an insight, just that their roles and interaction with officers from other unions was more limited, and where there was crossover between unions, discussion between officers were more likely to be around servicing and negotiations rather than the specifics of organizing strategies.

It was interesting to note that others working in the union movement who were most likely to share the organizers' wide perspective on organizing (although not necessarily the detail) were often those at the opposite end of the career ladder. As a result of their specific and strategic roles, some senior union officers were perceived to have a greater understanding than other union officers of the need to effect a cultural change within their organizations if the union movement were to grow and develop. In some cases, this led to situations where there was general agreement from those employed at the top and bottom of unions on an approach to organizing, which was not necessarily shared by union employees in the middle. At times, this has led to conflict and misunderstanding with union officers and made the role of organizer difficult, particularly when organizing was held up as a way of creating cultural change within the union. Some organizers are very well placed to become critical thinkers about the future of the union movement more broadly. This wider perspective is also enhanced by the fact that this new cohort of union organizers tends to be more mobile between unions than other union officers. For example, although some organizers were kept on by their sponsoring union at the end of their training, others went to work for a different union and have since moved through roles in a number of unions. One of the most striking findings of our research is how much more mobile organizers are than generalist officers, and many of them have worked in different unions in the early stages of their careers. In doing so, organizers have developed a significant understanding of how organizing approaches and strategies differ between unions. In many cases, the insights gained as a consequence have enhanced the motivating factors that caused them to become organizers in the first place. They have also reinforced the idea, heavily promoted at the start of the academy, that these new organizers would be a catalyst for change within the union movement.

One challenge for the academy has been to keep this forum for the development of critical thinkers as the training has become more routine and formalized over the years. In practice, even though the training material has become more structured, the academy continues to be an engaging forum for debating ideas because it provides a space for organizers from different unions to reflect on practice across the labor movement. Thus the argument is a nuanced one. Undoubtedly, over the years, the academy training has become more focused on promoting a "toolbox" of organizing tactics. But many of the people who undertake the training are intelligent, curious, and highly politicized, so the academy remains a place to exchange ideas and gain inspiration. As a result it continues to produce at least some graduates who want to try to think more broadly than the focus of their training.

Some organizers had more instrumental reasons for taking part in the academy. Many were aware of the difficulties of finding a paid job within the union movement. In Britain, the historical route was to spend a long "apprenticeship" as a lay representative before gradually working your way up to getting a full-time officer position. Even then, union jobs were often few and far between because when people got staff positions, they tended to stay in the job until retirement. The academy, however, opened up a new route for a whole group of people who never thought they would be able to get work in the union movement:

> I suppose for me the academy was, I mean it was like a life changing year in that as a trade union activist it was very unlikely that my own union was going to employ me in any sort of lay capacity and I can't imagine how I would have found employment in the trade union movement in any other way. (OA organizer #13, white male)

This was particularly the case for women and people from minority ethnic groups, who are seriously underrepresented in union jobs:

> I think the Organising Academy has done brilliant things, I think it's brought people like me through the door and I've stuck at it and love what I do. (OA organizer #131, black female)

> The Organising Academy actually gave me a ladder into the trade union movement, which I don't think would have been there otherwise. I tried to apply for jobs in the trade union movement before but...[wasn't successful]. (OA organizer #91, black male)

Many will be familiar with the description of unions as "pale, male, and stale" and the Organising Academy is to be congratulated for helping to increase (slightly) the diversity of union officers, but this has not just been a result of recruiting women and black trainees. Academy graduates have also gone on to have an impact on the diversity of employment practice within their own unions:

> When I came in I was the only black organizer and then slowly things started to change and the union started becoming a bit more diverse within the workforce. The majority of our staffing of black and Asian staff is still within the administrative role. One of the things I've done over the last couple of years is to get some of these staff involved in organizing, and it then got to a stage then where they were actually running their own organizing campaigns. As a result we've now got more black organizers. (OA organizer #131, black female)

While it is true that the numbers passing though the academy (to date around 240 in total, of whom less than 10 percent are from black or minority ethnic backgrounds) are small in comparison to the approximately 3,000 officers employed across the UK union movement, it has at least made some unions more aware of the lack of representativeness of officers compared with union membership as a whole.

Organizing for Cultural Change within Unions

As mentioned, one of the central aims of the Organising Academy was that the new cohorts of union organizers would be a catalyst for change. The intention was that they would kick start a cultural shift toward a more strategic organizing approach, and the first few intakes were promoted by the TUC—perhaps unfortunately for them—as the future of the labor movement. Consequently, this not only raised expectations, but also created a degree of resentment and cynicism from others working for unions—particularly those who had been around for a long time and had struggled through the difficult years of the 1980s when union membership dropped dramatically. The OA trainees in the first few years acutely felt the pressure of being heralded as agents of change but were also excited by the challenge. "I think it was really exciting," one organizer said. "The first year was amazing. It was a really exciting year but it was also a really difficult year" (OA organizer #104, white female).

The challenges were surely very real. These included twenty years of continual decline and a shift away from a shop-stewards-based movement to that of a servicing mentality with the promotion of "add ons" to union membership such as credit cards and cheap insurance deals. Clearly, the move toward an emphasis on organizing, which required the involvement of an active lay membership, also required a fundamental cultural shift for many union officials, some of whom were reluctant to change their existing methods of working.

Many of the established generalist officers were not involved in the discussions taking place around organizing or the decision by their unions to recruit these new staff whom they had been told were going to "change the face of the union movement." Indeed, there was little notion of a "turn" toward organizing at this early stage, and even in the more committed unions, discussion about developing an organizing agenda was, realistically, limited to a few interested individuals. It would probably be fair to say that the union movement had yet to begin to "talk the talk" let alone "walk the walk" in these early years. So the first intakes of OA trainees really did carry a lot of expectations as they took on their new roles and tried to fit into what was essentially still a predominantly servicing culture:

> I think it was somewhat disingenuously sold to people as organizing is everything and servicing is—well, you don't need to worry about that. That's why so many people walked in and got blown to smithereens because they were politically naïve. I think that did people a disservice. It didn't reflect well on the whole project which was of ultimate importance, but it inflated their aspirations, whilst at the same time allowing it [the OA] to become a target. (OA organizer #45, white male)

Immediately, there was a distinction set up between organizing and servicing roles that entrenched the views of many generalist officials, particularly in the early years, and as we saw in the previous chapter, it is a tension that remains. In many cases, sponsoring unions did not have well-developed policy in relation to new organizing strategies and did not really know what to do with organizers when they arrived in their unions following their training sessions at the TUC. Organizers described how they were ignored or left to find their own way sometimes with little management support. In other cases, they really were expected to reverse the decline in membership single-handedly and were given unrealistic recruitment (note, not organizing) targets: "I asked a question a few months into my OA year. I said, 'Look, are you actually interested in organizing in new workplaces where there is no union, or are you more concerned with getting the numbers in?' And they just said, 'Yeah, get the numbers in'" (OA organizer #39, white male). Combined with the fact that many organizers were young in comparison to the generalist officer corps (in some cases straight out of college), this reinforced their junior and subordinate status:

> When I was going into manufacturing companies with the officers, the officer would always introduce me and say, "Oh, this is one of our little organizers." It used to annoy me because I used to feel like I was demoted straightaway, I was a lowly organizer. And going into some meetings they would always ask me to take the notes and I was like, "Well, I am not there to be a bloody secretary!" (OA organizer #87, black female)

In these circumstances it was often difficult for organizers to make their mark or to have an impact on developing new organizing strategies that were acted on, but most struggled on regardless and took comfort from their fellow organizers on the training program. The relationships that had developed with other OA graduates helped to build camaraderie among a network of organizers who were also struggling with their new role. While many talked about how tough the training year was for them and that it had been a "baptism of fire," they also felt that they had managed to climb a steep learning curve, which had helped to strengthen them as individuals and prepare them for battles ahead. But to what extent were the OA trainees really agents of change within the union movement?

Firstly, it is acknowledged by senior TUC officials that even though the number of union organizers who have passed through the academy is relatively small, they are considered to have "punched above their weight."

Indeed, some have gone on to take senior positions within the movement such as Paul Nowak, previously director of the Organising Academy and now head of the Organisation and Services Department at the TUC, and Sharon Graham, director of organizing in the biggest UK union, Unite. Paul began his working life in retail joining the GMB union at the age of seventeen. He went on to work in a range of jobs, each time joining the relevant union and becoming an active union representative. While working for local government he heard the academy was recruiting its first intake and decided to apply. He was taken on by the Banking, Insurance, and Finance Union (BIFU), which underwent a series of mergers before ending up in Unite, where he was involved in organizing projects among young workers. After graduating from the academy, Paul went on to work for the TUC in a variety of roles before becoming director of the Organising Academy. Since then, he has been responsible for the expansion of the academy training program to include courses for full-time officials and lay representatives as well as providing bespoke training and consultancy for individual unions who are developing their own organizing training.[1]

Sharon Graham, now director of organizing at Unite, began work as a silver service waitress. In this job she led her first industrial action, ensuring that agency workers who were working alongside her were paid the same wages. She went on to work for the Transport and General Workers Union (TGWU) as a secretary but continued to be involved in recruitment initiatives, particularly when the first wave of compulsory competitive tendering for public services was introduced. Her roots remained in building collective strength to give workers the best chance of winning, particularly in low-paid unorganized sectors. A work colleague gave her the advert for the TUC Organising Academy and she decided to apply. She took leave from the TGWU for a year and was placed in Unison, the large public-sector union, while she completed the academy training. Here she organized hospital workers, among others, before moving back to the TGWU. Now Sharon heads up the national organizing strategy for Unite and manages a large team of around ninety organizers. She has helped develop the sectoral approach to organizing, which—as we saw in

---

1. We would be remiss not to pay tribute to Nowak's fellow workers in the TUC organizing unit who have contributed much to the development of organizing theory, practice, and teaching. These include Becky Wright, Liz Blackshaw, Alison McGarry, Carl Roper, and Paula Hamilton.

chapter 3—has had considerable success in organizing thousands of workers in the low-cost airline industries, meat processing, contract cleaning, and the logistics industries.

While Paul and Sharon may be the most high profile of OA graduates still in the union movement, the achievement of many other graduates is equally impressive. There was an overwhelming feeling from interviewees that they *had* made a difference in affecting some degree of cultural change in their unions, but that there were too few dedicated organizers to do what was really needed to turn things around. Overall, organizers were reluctant to claim huge success in terms of cultural change and most were hesitant in describing their unions as "organizing unions." Instead they talked in terms of gradual change, and "I don't think the union has understood it as yet." One organizer summed up the difficulties of "mainstreaming" organizing through unions when she said: "When I am sitting in front of officers and I'm talking to them about organizing, nobody disagrees with it. It's when it starts to change the way they do their job, that's where the problem comes" (OA organizer #50, white female).

Reflecting on their personal journeys as organizers and the tenth year of the OA, a number of organizers expressed caution that a note of complacency was beginning to creep into the ongoing necessity for unions to continue with a strategic organizing agenda:

> I think the officials are totally persuaded by it and the new officials that come on board get the organizing model, but I think over the past couple of years there's been a transfer back to recruitment being the most important. (OA organizer #104, white female)

> There's the fear now that we go backwards rather than going forwards…some of the practices have been exhausted and people get a bit bored of the traditional method of organizing. (OA organizer #131, black female)

This notion of "organizing fatigue" was raised at a TUC roundtable on union organizing in June 2009, in which senior organizers and policy officers from a number of unions acknowledged that "narratives of organizing" (Martínez Lucio and Stuart 2009) had, to an extent, become "stale." This was despite the fact that both the theory and practice of organizing approaches have largely failed to reach down to the majority of trade union activists in the United Kingdom. Cultural change at this level not only has not materialized, in many cases it has not even been considered. As we highlighted in the previous chapter, an important barrier to the wider impact of an organizing agenda is, in our analysis, the relatively low status role of organizers within their unions. This is a feature of wider questions about career development to which we now turn our attention.

OA graduates are selected for the academy on the basis of their high commitment to the union movement and their background as activists in trade unions or student or community politics. The emphasis on membership activism inherent within the training means that the role of the organizer is far more than merely recruiting members. The intention is that they inspire a greater active commitment from the lay membership and promote cultural change within union structures. For this reason, organizers' level of commitment to the trade union movement is paramount to the success of the program of reform of which the academy is the centerpiece. It is therefore important to consider the way in which they and their work is managed within their unions and how this affects their ability to affect cultural change.

During the process of recruitment to the academy, candidates are assessed to determine whether they have the necessary qualities, skills, and experience to succeed as organizers. The competencies that assessors are looking for include interpersonal skills, communication, listening, influencing, problem solving, leadership, and knowledge of employment and equality issues. The intention is to identify individuals with the capacity to develop as effective union organizers, and the process was viewed explicitly as an alternative to customary principles of recruitment within unions, which have emphasized a record of lay activism and service. Organising Academy graduates have often been expressly selected because they do not match the stereotypical view of a union officer, and the opening of the academy has been regarded as a means of infusing the trade union workforce with new blood. "We didn't want old dogs from the trade union movement who live it but who can't sell it," explained one union senior officer. "They're not a good example to youngsters, they're too boring."

As one would expect considering the overarching aims of the project, the graduates have developed many of the characteristics associated with professional employees within organizations. Graduates of the academy can be described as a professional subculture—they are specialists engaged in highly nonroutine work who tend to identify themselves with the content of their work (i.e., being organizers) rather than with their organization (i.e., their employing unions). This is further reinforced by the fact that they are more likely than other union officers to change jobs by working for different unions, something that was unusual until the development of the Organising Academy.

Research has regularly reported the difficulties that professional workers can pose for managers in the workplace (see among many others Mintzberg 1998). In expressing deeper loyalty to their profession than their employing organization, they can present challenges for organizations seeking to change their culture (think, for example, of senior doctors resisting organizational change). However, in the case of organizers, they display a commitment to the objectives of the cultural change process and see themselves as "agents of change." As we show below, it is the inability of some line managers and senior officers in unions to live with these high ideals in practice that can cause problems. We suggest that what senior officers desire in such cases is for organizers to display "contingent commitment," in other words, that commitment to cultural values is tempered with recognition of the constraints of the organization and is enacted only when expedient. This can cause frustration and tension among all staff—organizers, senior officers, and generalist officers alike—but organizers, as the most junior staff, are the ones who are generally left feeling overruled and unable to carry out the job they feel they were employed to do.

There have been a variety of tensions between the organizers, people developing and delivering the organizing training, and senior trade union leaders. At least in part, these have arisen because of the commitment of organizers to the espoused cultural values of the academy and of organizing more generally. In these instances, organizers' commitment to change can exceed that of some of their leaders. Such situations are similar to those in which employees show a higher commitment to product quality (for example, Delbridge 1998) or customer service (e.g., Schneider 1980) than their managers. Organizers' reactions to these tensions have been diverse and informed by both current and historical influences.

Despite the overall analysis presented in previous chapters that organizing practice in the United Kingdom has been largely dissociated from broader debates within unions about its end objectives, strong views about this emerged among specialist organizers very early in the OA program.

Debates frequently raged during training sessions and informal discussions about the more strategic aspects of the role and the argument that it should be focused not simply on boosting recruitment. As we shall see, this has caused tensions within unions, and organizers have faced considerable barriers in their roles. But it is important to be clear here that this broader vision of organizing was central to the emergent views of organizers as professionals with specialist skills and as agents of change. Over time, and as the academy training program has become more formalized with a focus on the practical tactics of organizing, these debates have subsided. But it would be wrong to suggest that they no longer happen.

While specialist organizers have developed a shared understanding in the classroom, they have sometimes met resistance when they have gone out to their unions to put the ideas of organizing in practice. In the early days, in particular, many clashed with their line managers, officers, and coaches because of differing views on how to operate in the field, specifically in terms of the approach emphasized in their training and what was expected by the sponsoring union. In more than one case the relationship between coach and organizer broke down completely over the relative importance of organizing or recruiting. In one example, the organizer had expected to influence branch structures and set up organizing committees while the coach had wanted her to engage only in recruitment activity. The coach explained that "the [unions] are most interested in getting the numbers up. That is the key objective when it comes down to it" (OA coach, P1_1).

Another of the organizers had similar problems with her coach who wanted two-thirds of her time dedicated to recruitment. She argued openly against this on the grounds that it contradicts the messages from the Organising Academy. She commented, "A lot of unions just seem to be paying lip service to organizing.... He [her coach] said to me, 'I don't care what they are telling you at the TUC. Too many people see organizing as an excuse not to recruit.' That is undermining me and I wasn't employed to take that approach" (OA organizer P1_1). Although this was a dynamic routinely encountered in the early stages of the academy, it is still evident today. Nonetheless, organizers are united in their conviction that organizing must take priority over pure recruitment and another commented that "the organizing agenda is more of a long-term thing. [But] we are always asked how many people we have recruited. That seems to be the key for other people" (OA organizer P1_2).

Organizers' activities have also, on occasion, brought them into conflict with senior groups in the unions, particularly when they have gone outside traditional approaches to recruitment. One discussed, with frustration, union officers who appeared committed to organizing, yet preferred traditional recruitment techniques, "One-to-one [recruitment] is just so inefficient. It is so much easier to get people [in the workplace] to do it for you." One graduate from the first year of the OA commented that

> I think that at the time a lot of unions were doing it because it seemed to be a good thing and it was the fashion to have organizers. And I think some people in [my union] did get it but the majority didn't—the kind of organizing that I'm talking about. Certainly my regional manager was under the impression I was there to recruit, get out and recruit, get out and recruit. (OA organizer #23, white female)

Her "kind of organizing" had brought her into direct conflict with her line manager and with other senior officers within the union and had been a contributory factor in her decision to leave that union and seek work elsewhere. Another graduate from the first year of the academy noted that the focus on recruitment had caused him problems. He explained how this contradiction affected his work: "We ended up going round these firms asking for access basically. And it was just a joke, compared to what I was learning from the TUC at the time, it was almost like I was in two different places" (OA organizer #39, white male). However, the rationale behind this tension was also clear and several organizers talked very eloquently about the pressures they faced: "Because there is that lack of understanding of organizing as opposed to recruitment, people tend to look at the resources going into it and the members coming out of it" (OA organizer #43, white male).

One academy organizer working for the shop workers' union, USDAW, recognized the particular pressures that confronted her union and the tensions that this provoked in relation to organizing and recruitment:

> I mean we have to recruit, we've always got to understand that ours is a very, very volatile sort of area, high turnover. And when you look at the volume—70,000 we have to recruit just to stand still every year. As fast as we recruit them in, so—one of the main parts of our union is recruitment. However, the way that we do recruitment has changed a lot.
> Interviewer: In what way?

Well the training that we offer as reps now, giving them ownership of their own workplaces. Getting them to do the recruitment rather than us...I think I do with the changes that are going on within USDAW at the minute, because of the organizing project I feel that we're probably one step in front of a lot of officials that have been here for a long time. Because that's all what's embedded in me, I know no other way than organizing, so I've not had to change. So again I think I've come into the union at the right time as things are changing and certainly I don't physically go out now and ask people to join the union. But my patch, the numbers that are coming into my patch must mean I'm organizing as well. (OA organizer #6, white female)

These tensions are by no means seen only in the early days of the Organising Academy, although perhaps unsurprisingly, they were most evident during that period. Since then, most unions have a more developed and strategic view of the role of organizing for their particular structures and contexts. As we have seen in the previous chapters, there are still clearly different trends in how the organizing role is managed, but these conflicts over the extent to which organizing work can and should prioritize recruitment over other forms of organizing activity are still deeply felt and present a tension in unions. Even a decade on from the launch of the academy, organizers are often still more committed to a broader conceptualization of organizing than many in their unions. This makes them a difficult cadre of professionals to manage but reinforces their idea that they need to keep "fighting battles" to promote their vision of "organizing unionism." One significant barrier to their ability to promote this broader change is their often very junior status within the union, and this is a matter to which we now turn.

Opportunities for Career Development or Promotion

In our survey of academy graduates in 2008, we asked respondents which union had sponsored their training year, and which union currently employs them (if any). We also know from the contact details (e-mail addresses) of those that we traced, but who did not respond to the survey, that many of these were also still working in trade unions. From this we can say that 71 percent of the 240 OA graduates were still employed in the union movement. The fact that so many have continued working for unions suggests that there is a great deal of commitment to the work that they do. In many respects, the finding that a clear majority of graduates have remained employed in the union movement is testament to the success of the academy in recruiting a new cadre of mainly young, and certainly enthusiastic, recruits to their ranks.

So what are the graduates doing now? Of those who responded to our survey and who were still employed in the union movement, around half are employed as specialist organizers, and the other half are in other roles. Those taking on other roles are, by and large, generalist officers undertaking the usual bargaining and representation roles. Some, however, are in wider policy roles such as training officers, TUC policy roles, senior national officers, and other key positions within the wider union movement. At least a third of the graduates who still worked in the union movement were no longer working for the same union that had sponsored them, which indicates a movement of trained organizers between unions. This is a considerable innovation within British unions, which previously had a tradition of recruiting internally, rather than developing a pool of skilled workers whose skills could be transferred between unions (Kelly and Heery 1994). Indeed, because of the competition between unions, in the past there was often a deep suspicion of recruiting people who had previously worked in other unions. This has very much dissipated over the past decade, reflecting both pragmatism that the aging membership base will limit the pool of potential recruits to officer and organizer roles but also reflecting a professionalization of the recruitment process more generally. In this regard, the academy offers a way into working in the trade union movement for people who cannot or do not want to move through the ranks in the traditional manner, perhaps because they are younger, or because they have relatively little experience of unions.

In many respects, the finding that a clear majority of graduates have remained employed in the union movement is testament to the success of the academy in recruiting a new cadre of mainly young, and certainly enthusiastic, recruits to their ranks despite the fact that the absolute numbers were small, perhaps 5–10 percent of union employees. However, as might be expected, not all OA graduates remained within the union movement. In some cases this decision to leave followed a realization that organizing work was not what they wanted to do or that they wished to pursue a different career. Nonetheless, many took their organizing skills with them into their new jobs. We found that a number of "leaver" graduates had moved into what might be considered "political" roles or organizing roles within broader social movements and social activism. For example, one graduate became a member of Parliament (MP), one now works with the Workers' Education Association, and another works in a very senior role within a voluntary-sector organization working with young people. Principles of social justice clearly remain extremely important to these leaver graduates.

As there were so few "leavers," we made a deliberate attempt in the ten-year evaluation project to interview as many as possible and what was striking about the stories we were told was that most did not see themselves as leaving the trade union movement at all. Many were still union members and active within their own unions. Others, such as the MP, actively worked to develop links with unions in their new roles: "I absolutely wouldn't consider myself a leaver. I really wouldn't...I see my role as organizing communities and that's what I do" (OA graduate #63, white female). However, it is also the case that a few graduates have left the world of trade unionism after some negative experiences of working in the movement. Although these graduates were a small minority amounting to no more than a handful, their experiences deserve some attention because they highlight some of the difficulties organizers can face.

Echoing many of the arguments and analysis in Rooks's data (2003, 2004) on US organizers, our findings indicate that for some leavers work pressure was the main cause of their decision to leave the union movement. In some cases, it was the pressure of the particular way in which organizing was managed in the sponsoring union that led to disillusionment with the role, or to a realization that it was not a role they wanted to pursue in the longer term. Many of our interviewees (leavers and stayers) noted that the role is often one that demands a great deal of time, commitment, and personal sacrifice. One graduate, who had subsequently left the movement, but who was broadly positive about his experience at the OA commented:

> I just didn't want to live out of a suitcase and not have any sleep, it wasn't for me. And just in terms of my personal circumstances, that year [training] had worked quite well for me because my wife stayed on at university for another year. So in a sense it was a year when I was footloose and fancy

free but then come the end of the year, we wanted to actually settle down together. (OA graduate #67, white male)

The reference this interviewee raises in relation to maintaining a personal relationship while undertaking organizing work is important. This is not an insignificant consideration for those taking on the organizing role in the union movement. A considerable number of graduates—particularly those who were required to work away from home—talked at length about the difficulties of managing personal relationships with husbands, wives, partners, and children. However, even those who were home-based often worked long, erratic, and unpredictable hours, which could lead to tension and conflict in relationships.

A very small, but important number of "leaver" graduates discussed the political challenges of working in the trade union movement in a very negative way. For a small number, the challenges of the role had brought them into conflict with powerful people within their unions, which had left them scarred by the experience. One who subsequently left the union movement felt very disillusioned with her experiences: "I got to a point where I had sort of to apply for jobs and really the thought of working for another union filled me with dread. And it got to the point where I wasn't applying for anything because I didn't want to work for a trade union" (OA graduate #84, white female).

We also heard some very difficult stories about how some graduates felt that there was a political agenda against the efforts at broader culture change to promote organizing and, by default, therefore against them, which links to a point we make later about the difficulties in relying on comparatively junior staff to promote organizational change. Some who had started to progress in their careers also made similar points.

I've made a decision now that I need to get out, and I'm not clear about [it], because I don't want to go into negotiating, I don't want to particularly— I'd rather go into policy work or I'd rather go into campaigning work. I'd rather get out of the trade union movement altogether in part actually because it's still such a boys' club. (OA graduate #27, white female)

We return later to the issue of trying to use academy-trained organizers to promote broader cultural change, but the central point is clear here: some organizers feel or felt that the responsibilities placed on them to change the direction and culture of their unions either personally put them in difficult circumstances or was simply too large a job for a small and relatively junior group of people to achieve. This raises important questions about the broader project of change that are important for issues of union renewal. Before we move on to consider these broader issues, it is extremely important to recognize the impact of organizing work on the lives of organizers outside of their careers. Our research is unusual because it allows for precisely this kind of comment, much of which was made without prompting from interviewers. This allows us to explore the very personal challenges and demands that organizing makes on people's wider lives, which again, is profoundly significant in relation to our broader argument that there are considerable barriers to promoting change through a comparatively junior group of staff.

Life Beyond Being an Organizer

One of the notable themes when talking to organizers about their work is the difficulties and demands it often makes on their home and personal lives. Many referred to either specific or hypothesized future challenges of balancing this kind of work with their personal circumstances. This is true both of the training year—which, at very minimum, demands frequent travel for the classroom-based training sessions—and of the jobs after graduating. For some, the logistics of the role presented difficulties, and most commonly, this related to the requirement to be nationally mobile and to the time pressures associated with this kind of work, particularly if they had (or wanted) children. And they often spoke very openly about the support networks they draw on in order to be able to do the role.

> I think the kids have had to grow up a lot quicker. Probably the academy came to me twelve months too early because I still had a son who was at junior school so he wasn't old enough really to look after himself. So for twelve months I had a childminder, the first twelve months—a lot of support. I found I had to rely on my parents quite a lot because my husband works continental shifts so although he's about a lot of the time, some of the times I have to rely on somebody else because of the shifts that he does. My kids have grown up now so I actually find it works better for me because I fit organizing round my home life rather than the other way around. (OA organizer #44, white female)

> I couldn't do the job unless I had that really good support system and by that
> I don't mean just being able to pay a childminder, you have to have family
> and friends that support you. And to be a good organizer you have to have
> that strong structure behind you, I think. (OA organizers #2, black female)

However, even the organizers without children noted some of the very real
tolls that their work had had on their lives. As recounted by a female organizer, "I got married three years ago, one of the reasons it took me so long
to get married was because I'm an organizer" (OA organizer #50, white
female). This point of view is reflected in how younger or newer entrants
envisage their careers. They often spoke about being unable to imagine
balancing the organizing role with other family pressures. One put it very
succinctly: "I am often finding myself thinking about I am twenty-five now
and at some point I would like to start a family and all that. And I don't
know how I'd do that as an organizer" (OA organizer #103, white female).

Confirming what has been described in many studies about women's
work generally (Hochschild and Machung 1989, Wharton 1994, and many
others), and women's work within unions (Heery and Kelly 1988, Kirton
and Healy 1999), these organizers have often had to be very disciplined in
defining their roles so that it has allowed them space to make decisions appropriate to their lives. And it is notable that there is scope for them to do
this within some unions, but this was in no way universal.

> For me as a single parent, when I think enough is enough and the day is fin-
> ished for me, the day is finished. I will not have my work phone switched
> on…and I advise people don't have your work phone switched on, have
> your own separate phone. When you've finished for the day, switch it off.
> Don't be contactable. (OA organizer #2, black female)

Some have been able to negotiate a more regionally based role for themselves and spoke very positively about it:

> Because hubby looked after the kids for me for the [training] year and then
> when I got back home, because I'm regionally based, I'm not nationally
> based. There has been, I think we did, we've done some things that have
> been nationally based but not very much. And I think people complained
> and said I want to stay—there's enough to do within the region without
> moving us around. (OA organizer #104, white female)

Putting to one side the specific difficulties presented by trying to manage the demands of a family life, others found that the work culture of (some) trade unions presented them with difficulties in their work. One spoke about it as a key reason why she sought work in another union: "I find that really objectionable that say a [union] organizer it was like you're hard drinking, you drink till three in the morning, you have no personal life. I mean how the hell are women going do this?...It was perpetuating a norm" (OA organizer #23, white female).

This takes us to a central aspect of our argument throughout this book: that the strategic decisions about how unions choose to manage and coordinate organizing activity has important implications for the objective of culture change within the union movement and for the lives of organizers themselves. We have outlined the main concerns of organizers in their daily lives and the links between those concerns and the broader objective of cultural change across the UK union movement. Important concerns relate to the junior status of organizing roles, the difficulties in balancing organizing work with other personal responsibilities, the intensive and demanding nature of the work, and considerable concern over the extent to which organizing can or should be mainstreamed within the work of generalist officers. Together, these raise an important question about whether or not organizing can be a long-term career option for those graduating from the academy. We now turn our attention to this question before making some concluding remarks about what these debates and tensions tell us about prospects for union renewal and revitalization.

Is Organizing a Long-Term Career?

Despite there being a number of high profile academy graduates in the union movement, there are very fundamental challenges to developing organizing as a long-term career. Among these is the common perception that organizing is an entry-level role and that many specialist organizers get "stuck" at this junior level. In terms of pay, organizing work is generally less valued than that of other generalist union officials. Almost all interviewees reported that pay was substantially lower than that of what they viewed as equivalent officer grades and this was a reason why organizers (often reluctantly) moved on to other roles within the union when they could. Further evidence of the underutilization of organizers' skills comes from the survey of graduates that was discussed in the opening chapter of the book. Thirty-nine percent of respondents with a specialist organizing role said they would like to use their organizing skills more. This indicates that a significant minority of organizers feel that they are stuck in relatively junior positions where they do not have sufficient scope to use the range of skills for which their training equipped them. This conclusion was further supported by interview evidence. Taken together, we can see that a significant minority of graduates are frustrated with the way in which their employing union understands and applies organizers and their skills. Specifically, organizing approaches that focus more on quantitative recruitment targets rather than building membership structures appear to be a source of frustration for some organizers. These organizers generally remain positive about the opportunities for their unions to change and develop, but the sense of fighting an entrenched culture is palpable, and they often see their ability to promote this kind of culture change as constrained by their junior status.

When they did receive "promotion" to a generalist office role, although organizing was no longer their main activity, many reported that they tried to incorporate organizing practice into their work and tried to use what they had learned to encourage lay activists to develop an organizing approach in their branches. This is an interesting development as it fits closely with the ideology of the OA when it was first established—the need to try to change the culture of unions at all levels, from lay activists to senior management.

However, it should be noted that there are relatively few senior organizing roles for experienced organizers to be promoted into. This also hides a problem in developing capacity, because junior organizers are generally not being trained and developed for senior specialist roles. An illustration of the problems of building organizing skills across the movement became clear in 2008–9 when a large union attempted to recruit a national lead organizer. Several rounds of advertising led to a very limited field of applicants suggesting that even when more senior positions are advertised, there are relatively few people with the skills needed to fill the role. This suggests that there may also be problems developing the skills and experiences of organizers so that they are capable of moving into such roles. This is perhaps not particularly surprising given that there are very few such roles to take on. Moving upward by moving into generalist roles is a more likely career path, so it would make sense for an ambitious organizer to seek to develop their skills in that area, but it does highlight the serious challenge of succession planning and developing a more strategic view of organizing.

Also important in these decision-making processes are the issues about balancing organizing work with commitments and interests outside work. Developing the points made above, for many of our interviewees organizing is seen as a "young person's game" that is a good entry point into the trade union movement, but unlikely to be a long-term career option because of the personal pressures encountered and the lack of promotion opportunities available. This has relevance to the broader project of union renewal because specialist trained organizers are frequently talked about as being agents of change within the union movement. If there are relatively few senior jobs and the talented organizers are not being brought into these roles, serious question are raised about whether the wider project of change can be achieved. It is to these broader implications that we turn in the concluding chapter.

Networks between Organizers

Partly in response to some of the challenges outlined in this chapter, organizers have developed networks among themselves to share experience and "best practice." In interviews, organizers often spontaneously commented on the ways in which networks had been established, and that they found these networks extremely positive sources of support, particularly in the early stages of their careers. Interestingly, the networks were both formal and informal, and served a variety of purposes that illustrate and facilitate particular aspects of the culture change.

Networks exist on many levels: within the individual unions, among graduate year groups, in particular geographical locations, and within particular sectors. Because many organizers are geographically mobile, their unions often ensure that there are formal and informal mechanisms for them to share information, ideas, and experiences. Most commented on was the very positive opportunity to have space to share experiences and ideas that was facilitated by the structure of the Organising Academy training year. A graduate from the first year of the program noted how unusual this was for unions and how challenging this was to the existing culture:

> One of the things about the academy—it took a long time to get there in 1998—was the thing about people being okay to talk about campaigns they were on. Because you know before it was like this—we've been told not to tell anybody and we've got to give it a different name in case someone's going to nick it [steal it i.e., try to recruit and organize in the same employer]....I mean, people were nervous about it, I was nervous about it because obviously you'd been told don't say what the bloody hell are we walking into here? But what was good is that none of us were going to go and take somebody else's campaign—it was never going to happen. So part of the breaking down of protection, the sort of defensiveness about this is our union, that's your union, is something that I think was flowing quite well in the 1998 academy. (OA organizer #24, white male)

But the following example shows how useful it was to the training experience and why trainees were so keen to continue to share information and experiences even if that challenged the dominant culture within their sponsoring unions:

> I think that the most useful aspect is when we're doing training, when you're part of a bigger group—the training is more effective. You have different views coming in, not just based on their experience in their current unions but also their experience before that. And also their general sort of angle and take on things. So that's useful. (OA organizer #28, white male)

One academy graduate now working with unions, but not employed directly by a union, commented that the training program was similar to Harvard Business School in the sense that it deliberately fostered relationships and networks that would be useful in the future careers of graduates. However, there is clear evidence that at the start, unions found it very difficult to accept a training context that relied on participants sharing their failures as well as their successes, for example, where a campaign failed to reach its objectives or where there were a particular set of challenges that could have been dealt with more effectively. It is remarkable that ten years later this is increasingly regarded as normal and even helpful. However, not all graduates have been able to keep their links with organizer networks as they moved into other roles within unions. One academy graduate who now worked as a negotiating officer commented that

> To be honest with you, when I went into that role one of the things that I massively missed was that…community of the organizers. Because the nice thing about [my union] is that we [organizers] do have that and we had regular meetings and gatherings between us, where we'd exchange ideas and everything. The negotiators don't do that and everyone operates in this little silo and they pretend that you know, well I've got more heavy workload than the other person…and you don't really seem to know who does what. (OA organizer #131, black female)

It is notable that the London area has by far the most developed networks available to organizers. This is not particularly surprising as most UK unions have their headquarters in London, and many organizers are located within their union's headquarters. This facilitated a useful cross-union exchange of views and information. The following view was typical of the comments on the London Organizers' Network: "The London network is really good because we do get the e-mails and know what's going on. And sometimes that would prompt me to send a message to [a friend in a different union] about what's going on, and I've heard this is happening in your area and stuff like that" (OA organizer #2, black female).

Yet outside London, there is much less evidence of these kinds of more formal networks surviving after the training period. Graduates living in Birmingham, Manchester, Scotland, and Wales all commented on how they would like to have access to the kind of support that their London-based colleagues have. The lack of such networks largely seems to be accounted for by the fact that there are far fewer organizers based in regions than there are in and around London, thus it is difficult to build up a "critical mass" of people who are engaged in such networks.

Conclusions

We clearly see the toll that organizing roles can take on people's lives both inside and outside their working lives. But why does this matter? First, it is important because organizers are central actors in the labor movement and within their struggles are the stories of the labor movement more widely. Understanding this is fundamental to our evaluation of the "turn to organizing" in the British trade union movement over the past decade. Organizers are, necessarily, central actors in this process, and if there are barriers to their ability to continue or progress in the role, to the effective use of their skills, or to their efforts to promote change, these have important implications for any likely prospect of wider renewal.

Our research indicates that there are many such barriers and that they are mainly a product of the way that the organizing function is managed within trade unions. There will always be tensions between the extent to which organizing activity is "mainstreamed" into the role of generalist officials or kept as a separate function within the union. We do not aim to comment here on the viability or desirability of different approaches (although see Simms and Holgate 2010a for further discussion), but we do wish to comment on the existence of different approaches that have their own advantages and disadvantages for organizers.

Employing specialist organizers has been the dominant approach since the establishment of the Organising Academy. The central advantage is to develop a cadre of staff with specialist skills and with the space to focus on building organization and membership. The potential difficulty is that organizers then become very isolated and tensions build between specialist and generalist officers. This can artificially draw lines around the start and finish of organizing campaigns, because having to prescribe a start and finish point at which specialist resources are invested leaves organizers without a clear sense of how a campaign will progress after their involvement. Further, this approach can create tensions between the perceived (and often real) status differences between specialist and generalist officers. Either organizers are a junior resource to be mobilized at the direction of the generalist officer, or they are more equal partners with different and often conflicting views about how to proceed in a campaign. Both of these approaches potentially cause tension and inefficiency. In response to the perceived lack of specialist career opportunities many organizers have moved into generalist roles. Although this undoubtedly gives them more flexibility for developing their careers, it risks depriving them and their unions of the application of the specialist skills in which they have been trained.

The approach of mainstreaming organizing work into the roles of officers is less common but is being experimented with by some large unions, notably the GMB (see the previous chapter). This approach risks pushing organizing activity off the priority list of generalist officers and reduces the numbers of specialist organizers needed within the union. But potentially the roles available for organizers are more strategic, more about training officers in organizing skills, and more integrated into the overall planning of the future direction of the union. This may be appealing to some unions and organizers, but carries the risk that resources will be directed away from resource-intensive activity toward whatever generalist officers can take on alongside their other roles and responsibilities.

It is clear that the "mainstreaming" approach may not be suitable in all circumstances, but it has a significant advantage that it offers career development opportunities for organizers. The lack of senior organizer roles is currently a significant barrier to the careers of the organizers we interviewed. An alternative approach might be to attempt to improve the status of organizing (and organizers) within the union structures by, for example, giving them equal pay to officers at similar levels, by developing a more strategic role for their skills, and by offering opportunities for progression.

Of serious concern for the project of promoting organizing activity more generally is the central finding that so many organizers experience a profound conflict in their personal lives as a direct consequence of the work that they do. This manifests itself in different ways, depending on a range of factors such as the age; gender; status of organizers; their commitments outside work, including, but not limited to, whether or not they bear the responsibility to care for other family members; and whether or not they are the primary income earners. But the central message is that they perceive the role to be a time-hungry one and one that demands a great deal of personal investment beyond a normal "job." For most, their career is a source of great pleasure despite the challenges, but the degree of burnout and the lack of career progression means that there is often little opportunity to develop other than by moving into generalist roles. This "organizing fatigue" is an increasingly common part of the stories being told both by organizers and policymakers and is of deep concern to those with an interest in continuing to promote organizing more widely. As Rooks notes (2003), the transformative potential of organizers within the labor movement is largely taken for granted but little work has been done on the constraints that they face in living up to this potential. It is clear from her work in the United States and our work in the United Kingdom that the barriers are profound, and often have as much to do with how these workers have to juggle and prioritize their working lives as to how organizing is managed as a function within the union. Retention of these skills within the labor movement is therefore likely to remain an issue and pose potential challenges as the labor movement looks to these organizers to deliver a future vision.

5

ORGANIZING CAMPAIGNS

So far, we have looked at the rise of specialist organizer training in the United Kingdom over the 1990s and into the 2000s, and how those ideas and practices have spread into different unions. We have also looked at the challenges of being a specialist organizer. But what has been missing so far is a discussion of the day-to-day *practice* of organizing. In this chapter, we look at organizing campaigns and how practices are applied at the level of the workplace. Our starting point is to make it clear how the practices of organizing are often specific to the UK context. This is obviously helpful to readers familiar with practice in other national contexts, but it is also important because much writing on and discussion of organizing take the US context as the main reference point. What we have consistently seen in UK unions is that as these discussions have transferred to a different institutional and cultural context, ideas about what organizing is, its purpose, and how it can happen have changed and been adapted. What we now see, therefore, is something that owes its beginnings and inspiration to what has been happening in the United States and elsewhere—notably

Australia and New Zealand—but which is distinct, different, and "fits" within a UK industrial relations setting. Many academics and trade unionists explicitly recognize these links but are generally keen to make important distinctions between what happens here and what happens "over there." An important objective of this chapter is not just to explain what is happening in the United Kingdom, but how and why it is different from organizing in other national contexts.

In explaining why UK organizing is different, we move into an important and interesting area. By comparing broadly similar phenomena in different contexts, we start to be able to build an understanding of what influences union organizing methods and outcomes. Why do British unions tend to use particular tactics? Which external and internal factors influence those choices? And what are the consequences of those choices? These allow us to build a deeper understanding of the dynamics of organizing, the micropolitics of the choices that unions, organizers, and activists make, and the outcomes of those tensions, debates, conflicts, and choices. This takes us back to the questions raised at the start of the book and particularly questions of how unions build power and come to represent some interests over others. The central argument of this chapter is that UK unions have generally focused on organizing at the workplace level. With some notable exceptions, there is comparatively little emphasis on broader initiatives, for example, sectoral- or national-level organizing. First then, our intention is to examine the nature of workplace organizing activity, before moving on to consider some of the examples in which unions have tried to coordinate efforts above the level of the workplace.

Targets and Objectives

So what does organizing activity "look like" in the United Kingdom? We have several important sources of data to address this question. Our observation of campaigns, discussions with organizers, and the surveys of union organizing campaigns carried out between 1998 and 2004 all help build a picture of organizing practice in the UK context. Survey data were collected on 238 campaigns, primarily through returns completed by trainees attending the Organising Academy, and additional returns were collected from those undertaking a similar training program in the

shopworkers' union, USDAW, and from a small number of paid organizing staff from unions who had stayed aloof from the academy, principally
the general unions GMB and TGWU. We also have detailed ethnographic
information from case studies of eight organizing campaigns that we followed in detail over a period of between three to five years, and of experience working alongside organizers throughout the research period. This is
also supplemented with interview data about the day-to-day working lives
of organizers and by working alongside organizers during periods of observation of their training.

Overall, the work of organizers can be divided into "greenfield" and
"infill" work. This is a useful differentiation as the two kinds of work are,
in practice, quite different. Greenfield work happens in workplaces that
have no previous history of trade unionism, and the primary purpose of
these campaigns is to build membership and activism with the objective
of securing collective bargaining rights. Infill work, by contrast, happens
where the union is already established and often has bargaining and representation rights. The name is potentially misleading as it may suggest that
the primary objective of this work is only to build membership numbers
(to fill in the gaps in membership), and in some places this may be the case.
But more typically, there is also a focus on building activism, developing
representation structures, and building the skills within the membership
base so that they are able to represent their interests more effectively. In
chapter 6 we return to the issue of the variety of different outcomes of
organizing activity and assess these objectives in much more critical terms.
Here, however, it is sufficient to make a working differentiation between
these primary objectives.

Using this differentiation between greenfield and infill work, it is important to consider the targets of campaigns. Part of the purpose of the
New Unionism initiative developed by the TUC in the mid-1990s was to
encourage affiliate unions to expand into new territories, and in particular
workplaces where employment growth had been strong but union membership has historically been weak, notably private-sector services. The
evidence here is mixed and tells a complex story.

Table 4 indicates that more than three-quarters of campaigns were targeted at the private sector, with the primary emphasis being on private
services. Industries that featured prominently included supermarket retail, banking and finance, telecommunications call centers, distribution

TABLE 4. Organizing campaigns

Campaign characteristics	Nos.	Percent
Year of campaign:		
1998	48	24.4
1999	48	20.2
2000	49	20.6
2001	5	2.1
2002	24	10.1
2003	36	15.1
2004	18	7.6
Trade union:		
USDAW	46	19.3
GPMU	31	13.0
ISTC	25	10.5
TGWU	19	8.0
UNISON	17	7.1
PCS	15	6.3
CWU	13	5.5
Other (N=19)	72	30.3
Sector:		
Private services	110	46.2
Manufacturing	73	30.7
Public services	51	21.4
Voluntary sector	4	1.7
Targeted work force:		
50 or fewer	18	7.8
51–100	30	13.1
101–250	54	23.4
251–500	47	20.5
501–1000	44	19.1
Greater than 1000	37	16.1
Targeted work places:		
1	105	44.7
2–5	78	33.2
5–10	23	9.7
Greater than 10	29	12.37
Targeted employing organizations:		
100 employees or fewer	27	11.3
101–200	24	10.1
201–500	44	18.5
501–1000	29	12.2
1001–5000	38	16.0
Greater than 5000	76	31.9
Union status:		
Recognized for collective bargaining	97	40.9
Not recognized for bargaining	137	57.6

(Continued)

TABLE 4. Organizing campaigns *(Continued)*

Campaign characteristics	Nos.	Percent
Membership level:		
0	71	33.5
1–10 percent	50	23.6
11–25 percent	28	13.2
26–50 percent	46	21.7
Greater than 50 percent	17	8.0
Organizer (respondent):		
TUC Academy Organizer	191	80.3
Other	47	19.7
Female	121	51.1
Male	116	48.9
Number of paid staff:		
1	63	26.7
2	86	36.4
3–5	75	31.8
Greater than 5	12	5.1
Weeks of project:		
4 or fewer	31	14.4
5–12	80	37.0
13–26	41	19.0
27–52	45	20.8
Greater than 52	19	8.8
Status of project:		
Continuing	176	74.3
Concluded	61	25.7

Source: Survey of UK organizing campaigns
Data based on 238 cases (there are missing values for some variables)

and subcontracted public services, as well as printing and packaging and light manufacturing. Most were workplace campaigns, targeting a single site or small number of workplaces, and most were directed at sizeable concentrations of staff, several hundred or more. The size of organization that was targeted varied substantially, but there is an emphasis on targeting large organizations that are likely to yield greater membership gains and whose managers are likely to be more receptive quite probably because they have a professionalized human resources function (Kersley et al. 2006, 120). The greatest concentration of campaigns was directed at organizations employing more than five thousand employees, and well over half were directed at organizations with more than five hundred employees.

In many respects this is a positive finding; unions are targeting the private service sector where membership has traditionally been weak. But behind this is a more cautious finding that emerged strongly from our interview data and the time we spent with unions; although unions are expanding into new areas of the labor market, these are areas that are closely related to traditional union strongholds. For example, retail banking has a long history of comparatively high levels of unionization, so it is largely unsurprising that the call centers associated with large retail banks are a key target for membership expansion.

When asked to evaluate the broader impact of decisions about how to target resources, one senior officer noted that the challenge of this kind of close expansion is that it can track unions into a rather cautious approach to selecting organizing targets.

> [One union] spent [a] huge amount of effort and resource organizing lots and lots of small manufacturing plants. Hundreds of new recognition agreements, literally hundreds of new recognition agreement—well certainly over one hundred new recognition agreements. But hard fought battles over fifty people here, seventy-five people there, one hundred people there, which—in the grand scheme of things is good. But I mean actually you're not going to turn round the decline in union density organizing fifty and seventy-five here, there, and everywhere. (Interviewee #20, white male)

The evidence reveals a certain degree of prudence on the part of UK unions. We do not, generally, see expansion into completely new territories, or what Kelly and Heery (1989) called "distant expansion." This approach reflects a degree of strategic targeting; unions are keen to target larger workplaces that have sufficient members to justify a potentially risky and resource-intensive organizing campaign. It is also logical that they may seek to mitigate the risk by focusing on workers who have similar characteristics to those already in membership. It is notable, for example, that supermarket chains are being targeted in the retail sector rather than the plethora of smaller high street chains. There are already strong agreements with some of the large UK supermarket retailers that allow the unions involved to apply the knowledge about those workplaces to new areas of the same sector. Similarly subcontracted public services are an area where unions are likely to have members who previously worked for the service when it was provided through public institutions. Those members are allowed to retain their union membership as they transfer to the new employer, and there are some limited protections for them and for their terms and conditions of work. Although many of the new private-sector employers have resisted extending union representation rights to the rest of the workforce, they do represent a logical opportunity for expansion into new territories. In general, it is undoubtedly the case that unions would have to expand outside these sectors if they were to establish the kind of membership density across the whole of the UK labor force that they enjoyed in the 1970s. But many unions argue that this kind of targeting, which focuses scarce resources on workplaces where gains are more likely, is both sensible and effective.

The other thing to note about the campaign targets is that they varied substantially in terms of their industrial relations arrangements and degree of prior union presence. In a substantial minority of campaigns the union was already recognized for collective bargaining and the primary objective was to raise membership and strengthen workplace organization. In just under 60 percent of campaigns there was no recognition for bargaining, but in a proportion of these cases the union had a presence and was commonly recognized for the purpose of individual member representation. It was only in seventy-three campaigns (30.8 percent) that there was no recognition of the union whatsoever by the employer. In a similar number of campaigns, seventy-one, it was reported that there was no prior union membership.

This shows clearly that one of the most striking aspects of UK organizing activity is how much broader it is than similar activity in some other countries (notably the United States), a view supported by our time spent with individual unions and organizers. One organizer who worked across different unions in a community-based role reinforced a point that we have made consistently in the previous chapters.

And a lot of the stuff that we learn [at the Organising Academy] is key skills and doesn't necessarily have to be put in one of those contexts. Plus we've got such different unions. For example, PCS [Public and Commercial Services Union] would do mainly infill work. And CWU [Communication

Workers Union] all their organisers are on greenfield campaigns, so communities. So it's a lot more about how you do your one-to-one communication, how you identify leaders, it doesn't always put it in the context.
(Organizer #103, black female)

We therefore argue that the targets of organizing activity tend to be
broader in the UK context than in the United States. This is largely because of an important difference between how UK unions and US unions
define their organizing work. Again it is useful to differentiate between
greenfield organizing where the union is seeking to establish collective
bargaining for the first time, and infill organizing where the union is trying to improve and strengthen membership and representation structures.
Greenfield organizing is much closer to what many US unions tend to
think of as organizing activity, but the context in which UK unions operate mean that in practice even greenfield organizing is very different.
This is partly because the legal context makes it much more difficult to
delineate clearly between organizing and bargaining activity and, because
of this, by the relative lack of clear definition of organizing activity in UK
unions. Specifically, the voluntarist tradition of British industrial relations
means that there has only recently been effective statutory recognition legislation—despite largely failed attempts to establish statutory recognition
procedures in the 1970s. Only since 1999 when the Employment Relations
Act introduced a process whereby unions could force collective bargaining
on reluctant employers, have unions been able to delineate between prerecognition organizing and postrecognition representation phases in the
way that US unions do. In cases taken to the Central Arbitration Committee (CAC) to adjudicate the legitimacy of the union's claim for recognition, there is a clear legislative process to follow. After demonstrating some
support for the union, a bargaining unit must be established and unions
must then demonstrate that they have support of the majority of workers in that bargaining unit. Majority support can be demonstrated either
through membership or, more commonly, through a workplace ballot. At
each stage, the CAC has the right to adjudicate, and if the union is successful in showing majority support, it may rule that the employer is legally
bound to engage in collective bargaining.

This process clearly has the effect of providing an underpinning structure to greenfield organizing activity. Expressing a wider view, one officer

now working in a generalist role, but who trained as an organizer, emphasized that changes in legislation had been the main driver for the development of greenfield organizing work in the mid-1990s: "It's the CAC procedure is the thing that allowed the TUC to get into an academy. So without that, to be frank, organising is an uphill struggle isn't it. So unless you were already in a recognised workplace you had no chance" (Organizer #71, white male).

If a union needs recourse to the statutory procedures, first it must demonstrate some support (typically around 10 percent of the workforce), then a bargaining unit must be determined, then majority support must be demonstrated. At each of these steps, it is quite possible that the employer may resist the union, and if a case proceeds through the entire process it is likely that the CAC will be required to make a ruling at each stage. However, this apparent convergence between UK and US legislation hides the continued influence of voluntarism on UK labor relations. The government, the CAC, and unions themselves all promote the notion that the statutory process is a last resort. In other words, by and large the unions involved in our research try not to use the recognition procedures, preferring instead to rely on organizing campaigns to build sufficient support among workers that employers concede recognition on a voluntary basis. This approach is formally supported and encouraged by the state, and it was never intended that the statutory processes routinely be used in greenfield union organizing. Further, even if a campaign does proceed to the first or second stages of the process, the CAC will actively encourage the employer and the union(s) to reach a voluntary agreement before the process is exhausted.

There is therefore a strong view among union officers and organizers in UK unions that they should avoid the statutory recognition processes where possible. This view is underpinned by several arguments. First, in common with the US National Labor Relations Board (NLRB) system, the process is slow and expensive—although not nearly as slow and expensive as the NLRB process. Being legalistic in its nature, the process often requires the services of expensive lawyers on both sides. Unions are, generally, only prepared to invest these resources where there is a reasonable chance of a favorable outcome. Employers' lawyers can often find ways to contest issues in an effort to slow down the process, although some organizers we interviewed reported that the CAC is increasingly "wise" to these tactics and will actively discourage this kind of behavior. Second, even a successful ruling from the CAC can lead to serious limitations on union activity. The requirement to bargain collectively only covers limited core issues; pay, working time, and holidays. Employers are only required to enter the negotiations "in good faith"; they are not required to conclude an agreement. And third, if a union loses its case before the CAC, it is automatically disqualified from reapplying for statutory recognition rights for three years. This is a potentially high penalty for unions and can act as a disincentive to pursue anything more than the cases for which a CAC ruling in favor of the union is very likely.

So, in greenfield organizing, it is unsurprising that the use of the statutory processes both directly and indirectly account for only around 20 to 30 percent of all recognition deals (Gall 2007). The rest are negotiated entirely outside the statutory processes. But a notable finding of Gall's analysis of both statutory and voluntary recognition campaigns is that only around 40 percent of greenfield organizing campaigns reach a successful conclusion, that is, establish a recognition agreement within the eight-year time period he studied (1995–2003). These findings are discussed in more detail later in the final chapter where we consider the outcomes of union organizing campaigns, but they are notable in that they suggest a central reason why unions are keen to define their organizing activity as being broader than simply greenfield activity.

Given that greenfield organizing activity with the objective of securing voluntary recognition requires that unions pay considerable attention to persuading employers to grant recognition, the objectives of these campaigns are slightly different from statutory campaigns. Far greater attention is paid to opening a dialogue with managers, identifying issues where managers can grant concessions to the union, and building worker support for collective bargaining. The tactics and methods used to achieve this are discussed in the following sections, but here it is important to note that the objectives of such campaigns are different. This brings our attention back to the fact that organizing activity in the United Kingdom can have a very wide range of outcomes other than simply recognition for collective bargaining. We therefore need to conceptualize the objectives of organizing campaigns very differently than has been done in the literature emerging from other countries.

We have seen that greenfield organizing campaigns are only one small part of union organizing activity in UK unions, and that statutory

greenfield campaigns are only a small subsection of greenfield organizing activity. We also briefly mentioned a "hybrid" arrangement that is not uncommon in the United Kingdom: that the union may have rights to represent individuals, but not to bargain collectively. Since 1999, UK labor law has allowed a positive right for any trade union member to be represented by their union if they have a problem at work—specifically a grievance or disciplinary case. This allows unions an important "way in" to a target workplace. Grievance cases are rarely truly individual issues; typically a problem at work is likely to affect more than one person. A collective grievance can therefore be raised, and the union has the right to go into the workplace to represent the members concerned even if the employer is resisting granting rights to collective bargaining. As one of our participants explained, this is an important lever. It gives the union legitimacy in the eyes of both workers and managers. If issues are identified effectively, it should be possible to gain a reasonable compromise on the issue of concern, thus reinforcing the idea of the union as an effective voice for workers.

There are, however, potential pitfalls with this approach. First, there is a danger of spreading officer time too thinly. If all members can demand representation whether or not there is a system of workplace representatives, the work in unrecognized workplaces will mainly fall to officers. Many unions have taken the view that this is unsustainable and have rules about how to access this service. In practice, this can mean that only members in workplaces that are a strategic target for establishing recognition for collective bargaining will gain access. Second, there is a danger that this tactic may go against the core principles of organizing, that members work together to address workplace issues. Again, most unions are pragmatic about this and argue that if a workplace is a strategic target, these rights are useful to gain access and to build relationships with managers.

The "hybrid" arrangement previously mentioned, where there is a preexisting formal agreement with managers that individual workers can have access to representation, but no such agreement to undertake collective bargaining, may seem odd to non-UK readers, but is again related to the notion that labor relations can and should be left to the parties concerned rather than tracked into a legalistic process. Typically it may emerge at the end of an organizing campaign that has failed to secure full collective bargaining, but where managers have agreed to individual representation rights. Some of these agreements are legacies from before the 1999 legislation that granted these universal rights. Others are agreements that then allow for a system of union representatives to take on this work, thus avoiding the pitfalls of the legislative rights discussed above. It is unsurprising that these workplaces feature as organizing campaign targets, because once a union has secured a legitimate representative role in a workplace, it is very likely that they will push to expand that role in future. These organizing campaigns mainly have the objective of increasing membership and strengthening representation structures so that a claim for full representation rights can be made at a later date.

Separate from these "hybrid" arrangements, around 40 percent of our surveyed organizing campaigns took place in workplaces where there were already formal rights to collective bargaining, so called in-fill organizing campaigns. We therefore need to reflect on the objectives of some of the wider in-fill organizing campaigns that form a substantial minority of UK organizing campaigns. These campaigns take place within both the public and private sectors. But the experience of public-sector organizing illustrates the kinds of campaign objectives that unions are seeking in these workplaces. The influence of the high level of public-sector union membership means that for many unions, organizing campaigns will take place in a context where even if employers are not supportive, it is unlikely that they will actively be trying to undermine the union. The particular history of UK trade unionism is such that unions regularly compete for members within the same sector. Thus, for example, although just one union represents university teachers, there are five or six unions competing for membership among schoolteachers. As a result of this sectoral competition, a large number of UK unions, both large and small, specialist and generalist, compete for members in various sectors and industries.

Organizing in workplaces that already have recognition for collective bargaining takes a very different form in the UK context than greenfield organizing, or even organizing in the hybrid arrangements discussed above. Many, if not most, public-sector unions have preexisting recognition and representation rights. Although some governmental organizations initially resisted union recognition, under pressure from the relevant union (PCS), these bureaucracies generally have decided to grant recognition as long as the union can demonstrate sufficient support, usually judged by membership numbers. More commonly, unions do not even have to consider their representation rights, and both managers and the unions operate in a comparatively benign context. Workplaces where recognition for collective bargaining is already secured highlight a final, very important, set of objectives: that of making union membership and representation structures more representative of the workforces from which they recruit. Groups that are usually involved in issues of representation are women; black and minority ethnic workers; young workers; workers with disabilities; and gay, lesbian, bisexual, and transgendered members, although it should be noted that the first three groups have certainly received the greatest attention among both trade unionists and academics. We do see a strong commitment in UK unions to increasing the membership and, perhaps more important, the participation of these groups in the decision-making structures of the union. But this hides an important issue identified in some of the case study research; women, black and minority ethnic workers, and young workers are all far more likely to be working in sectors of the economy that are unlikely to have a union presence. These workers are more likely to be working in retail, hotels and catering, personal services, and other sectors where unionization rates are low. In other words, the caution that many unions exhibit when selecting their organizing targets can lead them to fail to organize in the sectors that employ large numbers of underrepresented workers. Nonetheless, in many campaigns that are chosen as targets, ensuring appropriate levels of membership and representation of these groups is a central objective.

Methods of Organizing

Organizing methods fundamentally link to the purpose of organizing. If, for example, unions are seeking expansionist organizing objectives such as moving into new territories or workplaces where the union has not previously had representation rights, the methods and practices that they use to target new groups of workers are likely to be different from those unions or campaigns that seek consolidation or in-fill objectives. We therefore return to a point made previously that we are very critical of the notion that there is a single organizing "model." This is underpinned by and reinforced by the breadth of organizing activity in the United Kingdom. The notion of an organizing model has been critiqued and some authors conclude that it is an analytically unhelpful construct (de Turberville 2004, Simms and Holgate

2010a). Here, we argue that although there is certainly scope for critical engagement with notions of organizing, the organizing campaigns that we have empirically dealt with throughout this research undoubtedly represent a departure from previous thinking and practice within UK unions.

So what tactics do UK unions use in organizing campaigns? The campaign survey indicated that many campaigns run by UK unions were modestly resourced. Well over half had a single or pair of paid organizers working on them, and in virtually all cases involvement was for only a proportion of the organizers' working time. Intensive, heavily resourced campaigns that take place in the United States are a rare occurrence in Britain. This certainly fits our qualitative observations. Although there are exceptions to this approach—most notably the Justice for Cleaners campaign run by Unite in London's City and docklands areas (see Holgate 2009b for more details)—the most common approach to organizing is to have a comparatively small number of organizers working over a period of months rather than years. Most campaigns had been running for less than a year when the survey return was completed, though there were a small number of very long campaigns. Most lasted a few weeks or months, although it is essential to recognize that only a minority of campaigns (25.7 percent) had been formally concluded at the point at which the survey was carried out. Organizers provided information on recent or current campaigns, and in most cases union activity was scheduled to continue. It is important to remember this when interpreting the data.

Reflecting the objectives of recruiting lay activists and involving them in organizing, a majority of campaigns involve union members. Nevertheless, lay involvement is lacking in a fifth of campaigns, and in more than two-thirds there are fewer than five activists taking part. Higher numbers of activists are reported, unsurprisingly, where there was an established union presence at the targeted site before the campaign began. Involving activists in organizing their own workplaces is a key feature of almost all ideas around organizing activity and is an aspiration for most UK unions, partly because of the limited resources they have to invest in organizing. Making this aspiration a reality, however, can clearly be problematic, and this and other evidence suggests that the limited supply of active members can impose a constraint on organizing (Heery and Simms 2008). In some of the US literature it is argued that the inclusion of lay activists from other, fully organized sites is a particularly effective organizing tactic

Table 5 Campaign methods

Methods used in campaigns	Percent	Percent rated "very effective"
Individual methods:		
Direct mail/email to nonmembers	55	26
Subscription discount	43	33
Providing employment advice to nonmembers	53	24
Employer-dependent methods:		
Union presence at induction	13	50
Use of employer lists to identify nonmembers	57	81
Workplace meetings to promote membership	33	47
Face-to-face methods:		
Person-to-person recruitment at the workplace	83	62
Like-to-like recruitment	71	35
Direct recruitment by paid staff	83	41
Direct recruitment by lay activists	90	57
Organizing innovations:		
Rating of nonmembers' propensity to join	53	64
House calls to nonmembers' homes	24	40
Meetings away from the workplace to promote membership	78	48
Establishing an organizing committee among target workers	75	46
Use of grievances as a basis for recruitment	94	52
Raising the union profile through surveys or petitions	51	44
Link up with community organizations	18	24
Encouraging media coverage of the organizing campaign	27	29
Corporate campaign (e.g., use of shareholders/ customers to press for recognition)	12	15
High use of methods associated with organizing innovation	12	n/a

N=140 cases (there are missing values for some variables)

(Nissen and Rosen 1999). The use of remote activists in this way is rare in the British case. The fact that lay organization is typically tied to particular workplaces or employers means that it is difficult to transfer activism from established to unorganized union sites.

If the level of resources is likely to be one influence on organizing outcomes, then the methods used by unions are likely to be another (Bronfenbrenner and Hickey 2004). Table 5 shows both the frequency with which organizers report using particular tactics in campaigns and the percentage of organizers who had used a tactic who rated it as "very effective." Evidence was sought on the use of four broad types of methods: those that targeted individual workers (e.g., direct mail, subscription discount), those that relied on employer cooperation (presence at induction, use of workplace meetings), those based on face-to-face contact (e.g., person-to-person and like-to-like recruitment), and those that represented some kind of innovation in organizing activity derived primarily from the transfer of ideas about organizing from countries such as the United States and Australia. The latter comprised methods designed to build local organization and mobilize workers within the campaign (e.g., use of an organizing committee, identification of grievances) and those that extended activity beyond the workforce to seek community and wider support (e.g., media coverage, corporate campaigning).

All four types were used, although there are striking differences in the frequency of use and perceived effectiveness. Those methods that target an individual worker in isolation and seek to recruit on the basis of service provision are quite widely used but are seen by organizers as relatively ineffective. Employer-dependent methods, in contrast, are less commonly used, reflecting the absence of a relationship with the employer prior to many of the campaigns. Nonetheless, where they are used they tend to be rated as effective. Union membership in Britain tends to thrive where employers are supportive (Kersley et al. 2006, 114), and the survey evidence reinforces this message at the point of union building.

Face-to-face recruitment methods are among the most frequently reported. They also tend to be rated as very effective (see also Bronfenbrenner and Juravich 1998, 24), though there is a notable tendency for recruitment by lay activists to be regarded as particularly successful. There is also extensive use of some more innovative methods. Those tactics associated with mobilizing workers and seeking to build union membership around a core of workplace organization are both frequently used and seen as effective. Rating the recruitment potential of workers (mapping the workplace) and using grievances as a basis for organizing are regarded as "very effective" by more than half the organizers. Less frequently used are those organizing techniques that extend campaigns outward beyond the workplace. The use of community coalitions and corporate campaigning are especially uncommon. These campaign-extending methods, moreover, tend to be seen as less effective, possibly because they are used when the employer is particularly resistant to organizing. Coalition-building and other methods that seek to use power resources beyond the workplace are regarded as a highly effective organizing strategy in other national contexts (Tattersall 2010), but they do not emerge in this light in the United Kingdom.

One organizer highlighted these different practices in different national contexts and how problematic he felt it was to think about transferring a set of practices between national labor movements.

> I think the organising model that we were introducing for the academy is very much the American [and] Australian organising model. And I think that's where you got the resistance to organising from full-time officials and other parts of the union. Because people didn't like the idea of knocking on people's doors to get them to join the union and telephone canvassing. Turning it into a big campaign and in [the union I started work for] that's never been the way. We've never adopted that sort of direct method of organising. It's always been frowned upon. It's always had resistance....It's never worked and in a way we've tried to do bits and pieces. We try to ring members at home, we try to. [But] I'm never knocking on a member's door. [I've] been doing this for ten years. Never ever knocked on a member's door to try and get them. That wasn't the way. Maybe it might be more appropriate in different parts of the country but not in London....But in other ways we used, in terms of communications and using newsletters and e-mails and those sort of things to get people—petitions. Those sorts of traditional ways have gone down well in my organising experience. Rather than the very direct methods that they've used in America and Australia. (Organizer #91, black male)

Table 5 indicates that extensive application of any idea of comprehensive union-building strategy, that is, the use of seven or eight organizing tactics together (Bronfenbrenner and Juravich 1998), was confined to only a small minority of campaigns. Bivariate statistical analysis suggested that this comprehensive approach was a feature of manufacturing campaigns, those targeted at relatively low-skilled manual workers, and where there was no prior relationship with the employer. It was also related to union objectives: comprehensive union building strategies were applied where the aims were to secure recognition and build a workplace union with the capacity to deal independently with management. They therefore seem to be a feature of campaigns in more demanding contexts and also where the objective is relatively ambitious: to create a sustainable union presence rooted in workplace organization.

Again, the quantitative data are supported by our qualitative observations and interviews. Many unions have tended to use organizing ideas as a "toolbox" from which they can pick and mix individual tactics and methods. One organizer talked about how this approach was developed during her training.

> And so [organizing training] was very much on the toolboxes. Organising became a lot about mapping. No one talked about organising. They said, "Oh yeah. That stuff you do with the mapping." And not really understanding that that's a toolbox. What organising is about is driving workers' issues, hopefully sectorally, but driving workers' issues. And mapping became almost like well if you map, that's organising. Well, it's a tool to get to something we want. (Organizer #50, white female)

This reflects the particular way in which ideas about organizing moved into the United Kingdom in the mid-1990s. As discussed in chapter 2, the fact that it was the TUC that initially promoted organizing activity meant that it was necessarily largely not associated with wider political objectives. In other words, because the TUC has no direct jurisdiction over affiliate unions, all it could legitimately do was to introduce ways of approaching the challenge of renewal and particular tactics that might be used under the broad umbrella of "organizing." It is probably unsurprisingly, therefore, that there is little agreement on the idea of a single organizing "model." For example, one organizer noted how her union had adapted the idea of an "organizing model": "[My union] cherry-picked out of the organising model. They took what bits they liked and left the rest of it. So we didn't move from a servicing union to an organising one. And we haven't, we still haven't lost that servicing aspect" (Organizer #29b, white female). This, we argue, is central to our understanding of why organizing activity is a much broader-based approach to union renewal than it is in some comparison countries. There is less of an ideological commitment to the idea of one particular "model" of organizing than in some national contexts, and UK organizers seem more pragmatic about their use of particular methods. This reflects a number of important differences between the UK and US contexts.

First, organizing has been less associated with a particular political objective in the United Kingdom. The tradition of US "business unionism" gave organizers a strong political platform to propose an alternative "organizing" vision of trade unionism. In the United Kingdom, if it was contrasted with anything, organizing tended to be contrasted with "partnership" (Heery 2002). In essence, partnership was proposed in the 1980s and 1990s as a way of working closely with employers to secure mutual gains for the company or organization. As discussed in previous chapters, debates around organizing in the 1990s in the United Kingdom allowed space for a reassertion of the conflicting objectives of employers and employees. Beyond that, many of the wider political objectives of organizing in the US context have not been associated with organizing in UK unions. This lack of direct association with a political position is partly what has given UK unions the opportunity to label such a wide range of activity as being "organizing," and therefore opened the possibility of using a comparatively cautious range of tactics.

Second, there is a strong perception that UK employers are less hostile to union organizing than their US counterparts. This is discussed in greater detail in the next part of this chapter, and one of the consequences has been to push UK unions toward a view that organizing activity is much more routine here than in the United States. In other words, it is seen as being less necessary to build community support or to build support for the union outside the workplace. With a few notable exceptions, union organizing in the United Kingdom is largely workplace focused (Wills 2005). This, it is argued by some key practitioners, is essential because it is at that level that the institutional and legal support for trade unionism operates. This view that trade unionism "should" be focused at workplace level has a long history, which can be traced back to the formal separation of the political wing of the labor movement by the formation of the Labour Party in 1900. The fact that the Labour Party was created by, and largely funded by, UK trade unions to promote the political interests of working people was explicitly an effort to separate the political and industrial arms of the wider labor movement. Although it is arguable whether the Labour Party has actively pursued the political interests of working people in more recent times, this very early separation of the two functions has meant that trade unionism has largely been focused at workplace level since then. Wider campaigns, lobbying of parties, and coordination activities have, of course, taken place, but the main focus has historically been on improving terms and conditions of employment at workplace level. Given this focus on workplace organizing, combined with the wider pragmatism of UK employers, it is unsurprising that organizing campaign tactics have pragmatically focused so much on building membership and representation structures at workplace level.

Finally, we must be attentive to the training that specialist organizers receive, particularly at the TUC Organising Academy. They are very much encouraged to see the tactics they are trained in as being a "toolbox" from which they can pick and choose appropriate organizing methods. In no small part, this comes from the fact that the TUC is simply the umbrella organization of the trade unions. It is therefore extremely important that the TUC is not seen to be instructing unions how to do anything, let alone how to organize. This has created a context within which it is more politically expedient for the TUC to promote a "toolbox" of methods rather than a "model," which, by implication, may be seen as the one best way of organizing. This is also a pragmatic approach when the organizers being trained come from such a wide range of different unions.

These factors, plus the varying objectives held by unions, all help explain why the term *organizing* is used to describe a far broader set of activities— although typically a narrower range of methods—in the United Kingdom than in the United States. It should be added at this stage that it would be perfectly possible to argue that union officials in the United Kingdom have somehow "misunderstood" what organizing is about: perhaps that they are too timid in their application of core ideas, or what they are doing is somehow not "proper" organizing. In our view, this is an unreasonable criticism. We argue that their approach to what they are doing is certainly very different from ten years ago. At one end, the kind of tactics being used by Unite in the Justice for Cleaners campaign is very close to what is described in much of the US literature and has been consciously inspired by it. By contrast, for example, the work that USDAW is doing is also using many of the ideas that underpin notions of organizing. They are not simply recruiting members. There is a clear effort to develop membership structures, develop activists, and improve participation in the union so that members engage with the democratic decision-making structures more routinely. What differentiates these approaches is a spectrum of views on the extent to which organizing can and should be about promoting worker self-organization. We would argue that worker self-organization has never been as central to the political objectives of organizing in the United Kingdom as it has been in the United States. As a result, we see a far broader range of activities described as organizing by trade unionists. Nonetheless, as academic commentators it is perfectly reasonable—and arguably intellectually necessary—for us to comment on what organizing could seek to achieve. We look at that in the final parts of this chapter and in the final chapter, but before we do, we need to understand better the responses of employers to organizing campaigns, because they inform both the objectives and the tactics used.

A final point to note in this section, and picking up on points made previously about the issues relating to the underrepresentation of women, black and minority ethnic workers, and young workers in the decision-making structures of the union, is that we see very little evidence of unions trying to develop "new" ways of engaging these underrepresented groups. Some unions—most notably those that have actively sought to develop links with local communities—have experimented with efforts to attract young workers by, for example, having a presence at social events such as music festivals. Others have made an effort to link in with community organizations in areas where particular ethnic minority communities live and work (Holgate 2004b, Holgate and Wills 2007). And some unions have taken the issue of supporting migrant workers very seriously. But these have generally been the exception rather than the rule. The majority of organizing campaigns have retreated to organizing tactics that focus at workplace level and rely on networks and representational groups such as committees to engage these members. We have seen little, if any, discussion about whether existing union representation structures are appropriate to represent an increasingly diverse workforce, a topic that is returned to in the following chapter.

Employer Responses

Having established the broad approach of unions to organizing activity, it is important to examine the response of employers to these initiatives. We have already explored some of these issues elsewhere (Heery and Simms 2008) but feel that it would be remiss not to include some discussion of the importance of employer responses in this discussion. As mentioned previously, employer responses to union organizing in the United Kingdom tend to be less systematically antiunion than US employers are portrayed to be. Certainly a UK union would not necessarily assume that a target employer would, for example, hire a union busting consultant, employ delay and diversion tactics, or even fight a case through the statutory recognition procedures. In part, this reflects a broader business culture that has tended to accept a diversity of stakeholder interests in managerial decision making. But it also reflects a pragmatism in which businesses understand that although unions do tend to make material improvements in terms and conditions of employment, the UK union wage markup is significantly lower than in the United States (Blanchflower and Bryson 2004). Health care provision—a key cost for most unionized employers in the United States—is provided free at the point of delivery to all UK residents through the National Health Service. Other social security benefits in the United Kingdom, like sick pay for example, rely far less heavily on employer provision than in the United States. And unions certainly do not have the kind of political and social influence that they did in the 1970s.

Table 6 shows organizer reports of employer responses to campaigns, with figures given for all campaigns, those where the union was recognized for collective bargaining and those where the union was either totally unrecognized or had only a marginal presence in the employing organization. Perhaps the most striking finding for a non-UK readership is the fact that positive responses to union organizing are fairly common and are reported more frequently than negative responses. Faced with union organizing activity, a considerable proportion of UK employers have allowed organizers access to the workplace and to new employees undergoing induction, provided lists of employees and rooms and equipment, and have allowed lay activists paid time off to undertake recruitment. In about a quarter of cases, the employer has encouraged workers to join the union.

Comparison of columns two and three of the table, however, indicates that these positive responses are three to four times more common in campaigns where the union is already recognized for collective bargaining. They can occur where the union is weak or absent, but positive employer support is primarily a feature of in-fill campaigns, where the union is accepted by the employer and the latter presumably sees benefit in maintaining the level of membership and representativeness of its union partner.

The lower rows of the table report the frequency of hostile employer responses to union organizing campaigns. They indicate that many UK

TABLE 6. Employer responses to organizing campaigns (percentages)

Employer response	Union recognized N=97	Union not recognized N=139	All N=236
Positive responses:			
Provision of employee list	62.9	12.9	33.8
Allowing organizers access to the workplace	93.8	31.7	57.4
Encouraging workers to join the union	40.2	10.9	23.5
Allowing use of facility time for recruitment	67.0	15.8	36.7
Providing union with rooms or equipment	81.4	21.6	46.0
Permitting union presence at induction	61.9	11.5	32.5
Negative responses:			
Threat of legal or police involvement against union	4.1	20.9	13.9
Denying organizers access to the workplace	8.2	63.3	40.5
Discouraging employees from joining the union	11.3	61.2	40.5
Distributing antiunion literature	4.1	24.5	16.0
Victimization of union activists	7.2	34.5	23.2
Improving pay and conditions to reduce demand for union membership	3.1	23.0	14.8
Setting up or strengthening alternative channels of worker participation to substitute for union	10.3	52.5	35.0
Use of a management consultant to advise on avoiding unionization of the workforce[1]	0	22.1	12.9

[1] This question was added in the later years of the survey reflecting growing concern about the role of consultants, N=178

Source: Survey of UK Organizing Campaigns

employers seek to block unionization and that this is particularly a feature of greenfield campaigns, directed at sites where the union is absent or has only a weak presence. Negative responses are reported five or six times more frequently in this type of context than they are for in-fill campaigns. Although resistance is common, more than half the organizers report none of the responses. Even for greenfield campaigns there are only three negative responses—denying access to organizers, discouraging joining, and setting up or strengthening a nonunion channel of representation—that are reported by a majority. Employers in Britain can be ruthless in resisting unionization but the extent, degree, and sophistication of antiunionism appear less than those seen currently in the United States (see Bronfenbrenner and Hickey 2004, 39).

Nonetheless, table 6 indicates that UK employers have sought both to "suppress" and to "substitute" for trade unionism (Blyton and Turnbull 2004, 302). Many examples of union suppression were gathered through the qualitative research, which embraced refusal of access to organizers, threats of company closure, monitoring of workers, and threatened or actual dismissal of activists:

> I would like to highlight that management were extremely hostile. There are surveillance cameras at the only entrance of the building. Staff were afraid to even stop and speak to us at the gate. Management had previously sacked the last employee who spoke about getting a union. This happened four years ago and was still in the forefront of people's minds. (USDAW organizer, P1_3)

> The company employs a high percentage of Asian workers whose first language is Gujarati. When we first started the campaign, factory-gating, the factory manager, who is Asian, called all the Asian workers together on the shopfloor and told them that he would sack anyone who joined the union. That week, he phoned them all at home and told them again that they would be sacked. (KFAT organizer, P1_6)

There are also plentiful examples of union substitution, to improve working conditions in the hope that this would head off demands for unionization. These included removing unpopular managers, giving commitments to improve management operations, raising pay and benefits, and setting up nonunion consultative committees, the latter being a lawful response in the United Kingdom.

Beyond suppression and substitution two other hostile employer responses emerged from the qualitative research: attempts to forestall unionization through delays, what Gall (2004b, 44–46) has labeled "awkward stuff"; and attempts to undercut campaigns by inviting in a second, more compliant union, what Gall has labeled "tame stuff." Campaigns conducted before the statutory recognition procedure was established were frequently blocked by employers who refused to meet the union until the law was in place, while subsequently some employers have queried the application of the statutory procedure (Moore 2004). Inviting other unions to recruit has been a problem in a significant number of campaigns and reflects the absence of clear union jurisdictions in much of the UK economy:

> Currently recognition is under discussion, with some positive possibilities but the manager has "invited staff to join another union"—believed to be MSF.... Simultaneously with our recognition discussion a consultative committee is being elected. The latter we can handle, the former is more difficult—another union presence would confuse issues and make recognition far more complex. (TGWU officer, P1_4)

> After weeks of organizing and getting a substantial membership, other unions approached the company and offered to talk and arrange an "agreement." I have been told they are talking to five other unions (some with no membership). We currently have 50 percent membership. The company have told us they will choose a union they can work with. (ISTC officer, P1_5)

A final hostile response that warrants discussion is the use of antiunion consultants. Employers in Britain use these much less frequently than in the United States, but according to organizers, they have been used in about a fifth of greenfield campaigns. Notable examples from the early years of the Organising Academy have been the use of the American Burke Group by T-Mobile and Amazon to counter campaigns by Connect/CWU and GPMU respectively (Logan 2008). These were classic union-busting campaigns that were costly, sophisticated, and effective. In other contexts, UK-based consultants provided by law firms or employers' associations have been used without the full panoply of US antiunion campaigning. Indeed, what emerges from the UK evidence is the relative lack of sophistication of much employer antiunionism. It is often visceral, unplanned, and according to organizers, occasionally counterproductive, driving workers to the union. It is also not unusual for employer policy to change in the course of a campaign and become less hostile either because managers are replaced or simply learn more about the implications of recognition.

So, UK employers certainly have the potential to react with extremely hostile tactics but do not do so routinely. We argue that because of the dynamic processes involved in union organizing, this informs both union objectives and methods. Because UK unions operate in an environment in which employers exhibit a wider range of responses than the environment in which US unions operate, it further reinforces the idea that there is a "toolbox" of organizing tactics that can be deployed as required to secure a range of different objectives. If an employer is more hostile than anticipated during, say, a recognition campaign, it is quite possible that a union may agree an arrangement whereby they have rights to represent workers with problems, but they may forego the right to bargain wages collectively. Indeed, in one of our in-depth cases this was precisely the arrangement that was reached. For the union involved it was clearly hoped that this would be a step toward securing full collective bargaining rights at some stage in the future. But officials were clear that was unlikely to be an objective achieved in the short term. The deal was justified by the notion that representing workers on some issues was more desirable than not having any union presence in the organization. In this situation, the union had not anticipated that the employer would resist the campaign quite as strongly as it did. They had hoped that by focusing on key, larger workplaces, building support and membership, and then asking for a voluntary recognition agreement, the employer would concede to collective bargaining and full representation rights. The employer argued that the comparatively high levels of membership in the larger workplaces did not demonstrate wide support of the union because there were hundreds of workers in very small workplaces (often only one or two people) who were not members. With the employer refusing to grant a voluntary recognition agreement, the union could have pursued a statutory agreement but was advised that it was quite probable that the bargaining unit would be set as only covering the workers in the larger workplaces. This would have split the workforce into two; those for whom the union bargained collectively, and those who had no such rights. This was unacceptable to the union, and the alternative—to try to organize hundreds of tiny workplaces—was deemed too risky and too resource intensive. Thus the union agreed to a compromise whereby they accepted the right to represent individuals and to build a representation network, from which they hope to build enough support and membership to pursue their objective of securing full bargaining rights in the future.

This kind of arrangement, while not the norm in UK labor relations, is certainly not unique. In another case we studied in some considerable detail, the employer—a charity—persuaded the union to agree not to negotiate on pay levels but rather to focus on ensuring fairness in the mechanisms of pay determination (specifically how bonuses were allocated) and on bargaining over other terms and conditions. This was agreed because the employer was extremely concerned about the potential for the union to push up wages beyond the charity's ability to pay. The union was prepared to accept this unusual arrangement because the charity had comparatively little control over its income levels, and the issue of the absolute levels of pay was not a key concern for members; for them, perceived unfairness in the allocation of bonuses was a far bigger issue.

These examples are important for two reasons. First, they illustrate the dynamics of the decisions in relation to organizing tactics, and how those dynamics are influenced not just by unions but by the responses of employers as well. This point is surprisingly underexamined in previous discussions of union organizing. Often the employer is the silent participant in the background of many organizing stories. We strongly believe that we can only understand organizing activity if we pay attention to the role of employers. Employers' behavior is clearly influenced by the context in which they operate, including, but not limited to, laws, history, background, labor markets, product markets, company strategy, personal views and beliefs of managers, sectoral and industry traditions and conventions, corporate culture, and the behaviors of unions and employees. If we see union organizing activity as a dynamic process, then the politics of the decision-making process of both unions and employers need to be examined before we can understand the outcomes that we observe.

Second, these examples show that many organizing campaigns in the United Kingdom can result in hybrid outcomes; in other words, outcomes that are somewhere between full collective bargaining rights and no collective representation at all. This is in marked contrast to many US organizing campaigns where employer resistance would force the majority of greenfield organizing campaigns into a statutory process. Although most unions would probably argue that full collective bargaining rights are the preferred outcome of any campaign, employer responses are a considerable influence on whether or not this can be achieved. In the UK context, unions are prepared to accept some of these alternative outcomes either as a (hoped) interim measure, or as a realistic compromise that ensures that there is a union presence in those workplaces. Clearly, this links directly to our reflection on the breadth of organizing outcomes seen in the United Kingdom that is the focus of the following chapter.

Coordination of Organizing Activity

So far, this chapter has focused on organizing activity at the workplace level. Clearly, however, workplace organizing activity cannot happen in a vacuum, so it is also important to acknowledge the role of the central union in coordinating campaigns. Sherman and Voss (2000) argue that in the US context, organizing work is an important example of central union structures promoting innovation and activism at workplace level, in direct contradiction to the inevitability of Michel's "iron law of oligarchy" (Michels 1915). It is notable how long it has taken UK unions to develop a coordinated organizing strategy. In part, this is because UK unions needed time to understand how organizing activity might take place within the UK context. However, it also reflects the comparative lack of strategic planning around organizing issues in the mid-1990s. Added to this, as we argued in the previous chapters, the relatively junior position of many organizers means that it can be difficult for them to influence the strategic direction of the union, and tensions that can emerge between specialist organizers and generalist officers made it difficult to operationalize strategic plans in the early stages of the research period, even when those plans were relatively formalized.

Our early survey work (see, for example, Heery et al. 2000a) indicated a degree of formalization of union policy in this area as compared to the mid-1980s, when Mason and Bain (1991) undertook research that concluded that union policy in the area of recruitment and organization was very underdeveloped. Our 1998 survey indicated that the vast majority of UK unions had relatively well-developed national policies and monitoring process by the late 1990s. However, the existence of formal policies and monitoring processes does not tell us a great deal about the content of those policies, nor how they are implemented in an individual campaign. Our qualitative case study work shows clearly that although workplace campaigns are typically launched within the context of a national strategy, relatively little attention is paid to linking up union activity in different workplaces. Following arguments made in previous chapters, it is clear that union policies and structures play a crucial role in ensuring both positive and sustainable outcomes of organizing campaigns. Union structures that facilitate a flow of information and expertise between workplace and regional/national level appear to facilitate more sustainable outcomes by allowing scope for campaigns to benefit from the guidance and expertise of officials, while simultaneously developing the necessary skills among workplace activists. By contrast, campaigns run either from "bottom-up" or "top-down" can lack these features.

Our case study research shows a clear difference between unions relating to the effectiveness of the central union in allocating resources and commitment to recruitment and organizing activity in individual workplaces. In USDAW, for example, paid officials and organizers largely undertake this activity. The central union has considerable control over the work priorities of these staff, and they are routinely assessed against agreed targets and objectives. Targets, although not always quantitative, are always expressly set in consultation with senior officials at the regional level. Senior regional officials then, in turn, set targets in consultation with national officials. There is considerable scope as to how individual officials and organizers achieve these objectives, and there is scope for reassessing objectives if necessary, but the process is clearly and explicitly managed. This process of allocating the necessary resources to recruitment and organization is a crucial one, as it is a risky activity for the union to undertake, even where the employer is supportive. It is not a perfect process. Some officials, organizers, or even regions are more skilled at recruitment than others, and those who are less skilled are encouraged to seek training and support. Further, the union may face greater resistance from local managers or the workforce in some stores than in others. These factors help explain variation in membership between workplaces or between regions. Nonetheless, the effectiveness with which the organizing process is coordinated and managed from the senior levels of the union appears to have a considerable impact on the outcomes observed. In other words, there is evidence to support arguments that the process of coordinating organizing within unions can facilitate very effective organizing outcomes (Voss and Sherman 2000, Simms 2007a).

Conversely in some other unions, the process of coordinating and managing organizing activity at higher levels of the union was more problematic. In one of our case studies, we looked at a campaign by the PCS that aimed at a national target. Here, the union had few mechanisms through which to encourage regional officials to prioritize this work. The allocation of dedi-cated resources from the national union (largely in the form of organizers' time) went some way toward addressing this, but these organizers had a wide range of other responsibilities and had few resources to, for example, visit local workplaces on a regular basis. The union therefore relied heavily on recruiting and organizing methods that involved minimal time spent in the workplace and encouraged workplace representatives to take on most of this responsibility. However, they were poorly equipped to do so, often with little training and little previous trade union experience. This ap-proach has demonstrated some returns with membership density averaging at between one half and one third of the workforce. But as the senior official responsible for organizing pointed out, this approach had not delivered an effective and robust union structure in the face of difficulties for members (redundancies). PCS has largely learned from these early campaigns and now has a more sophisticated structure for coordinating organizing activity.

One senior national officer from another union highlighted how chal-lenging it is in practice to achieve a productive balance between workplace engagement and effective coordination of organizing activity. He empha-sized that the particular history and politics of the individual union was extremely important to consider when planning and implementing a new organizing strategy.

> So, the idea was—we need a structure first of all that puts the regions in control of the national office. That was the battle to win. Where the ability of the national office to launch a new campaign every week or month was curtailed. And we needed a structure that decided, on the basis of collective responsibility, which projects we would be pursuing and which we would not. Also we needed a structure that would allow the regions to come to a collective view on what things weren't working, what would never work and we should stop, and what things do work that we all know work gen-erally in every region and we should continue. The answer to all that was the national organising team as a collective body. [And] a senior person who has the ear of the General Secretary in every region to come together to do all those functions—so [that] the regions were bound into the decision mak-ing of the organising team. (Interviewee #4, white male)

This quotation highlights how difficult it is to balance and coordinate the interests of national, regional, and workplace union structures. To some degree, this has always been a challenge for unions. But the emphasis that organizing debates put on engaging members at all levels of the union arguably brings these potential tensions into even sharper focus than other activities.

Although all of the campaigns we studied had some degree of success in recruiting members and in improving workplace representation structures, there is considerable evidence that *sustaining* these gains is significantly more challenging. In line with many US studies (Fiorito et al. 1995, Bronfenbrenner 1994, Banks 1991), our case study research shows that the most effective campaigns are the ones that have both strong support from officials *and* strong workplace support. The campaigns that have support from above and below have tended to produce strong and growing membership and representation structures. By contrast, those initiated by the central union can have more difficulties building workplace support, which becomes a vicious cycle as the union becomes further unable to demonstrate its effectiveness at improving working conditions. There were also examples of campaigns generated largely as a result of workplace concern over a number of issues ("hotshops"). These have also proved difficult to sustain as the central union has been unable to manage an effective transition between the "organizing" and "representation" once the issues causing concern have been resolved.

Thus we argue that organizing campaigns are most effective when there is demand from workers for union representation, combined with strong central guidance and expertise. When one is present without the other, it is difficult to sustain workplace structures while transitioning into the "representation" phase of the campaign. Not only does this strongly support quantitative findings (Fiorito et al. 1995), the qualitative approach gives insight into why this is. The experience and expertise of officials and organizers in identifying collective, "winnable" issues is crucial. Inexperienced members rarely have the necessary skills to manage a complex and lengthy campaign without the support of union professionals. Further, the resources allocated by the central union are vitally important to securing sustainable outcomes, as the most effective campaigns are the ones that have had access to continued resources and a consistent approach during the transition to the "representation" phase.

At an aggregate level, one senior officer with responsibility for developing organizing strategy within his union stressed the political and financial importance of building sustainable organizing outcomes:

> So it takes time to grow your own in a way which is serious and sustainable. But, the other thing is that as part of developing capacity you also need to recognise the test, ultimately because you can't avoid the issue of membership. Because we have to deal with cynics and critics within [the union movement] and you can't avoid the test of membership. . . . [Y]our narrative also mustn't just focus on headline figures. Even with headline figures if you organise in the right way you will have a much more sustainable membership and the payback in financial terms is that much greater. Your narrative also has to focus on what you are achieving in terms of power for workers. (Interviewee #6a, white male)

At the workplace level, it appears that no matter how important a campaign is to the union's membership strategy, it will struggle to establish representation structures if it is unable to demonstrate its effectiveness. These findings link together the findings from several existing studies (Findlay and McKinlay 2003, Fiorito et al. 1995, Markowitz 2000) to give a clearer understanding of the dynamic processes at work during organizing campaigns. Equally, there is no consistent evidence from our research that indicates support for Fairbrother's thesis (Fairbrother 2000a, 1989) that worker mobilization is in and of itself sufficient to produce renewal in the trade union movement. Indeed, this research strongly indicates that the support of the central union is vitally important in establishing workplace unionism in previously unorganized areas. Although this evidence does indicate that *without* worker collectivism at workplace level, unions struggle to demonstrate their effectiveness and thus struggle to establish effective representation structures, this is different from arguing that this alone is necessary to promote renewal.

Conclusions

Our purpose in this chapter has been to give an overview of organizing campaigns. We can see that there is a considerable degree of caution in the targeting of organizing activity by UK unions, and we will comment on the consequences of that approach in the final chapter where we try to evaluate the wider impact of organizing initiatives since the launch of the TUC Academy. What is important here is that unions have not generally used campaigns to expand membership into new areas. They have focused far more on building membership strength in sectors and workplaces with existing membership, even in their greenfield organizing work. Unsurprisingly in light of the analysis presented in earlier chapters, there has been a tendency for unions to pick and choose between organizing tactics without an embedded commitment to using a bundle of tactics in what has been described elsewhere as the "organizing model." Equally, there is a deep commitment to engaging workplace activists, and if we were to identify a single feature that unites all organizing activity in the United Kingdom, it would be the concerted effort to involve workplace activists. As we have seen in chapter 3, what this hides, however, is a very large variety of different approaches as to how this might be achieved and what it means in practice. The range of organizing tactics used is partly explained within a context where UK employers are not routinely hostile to organizing campaigns. Unions are allowed access to workplaces in nearly 60 percent of the campaigns we surveyed, although in far fewer cases are employers prepared to support the union more actively. Although there is evidence of union busting spreading to the United Kingdom, it is not the most common reaction of UK employers. This is important because it explains why unions have not been forced to develop more intensive strategies to counter employer hostility.

We also see case study evidence that the campaigns that are able to produce the most sustainable outcomes tend to be those that are able to secure strong workplace activism within a broader context of the national or regional union coordinating the allocation of resources, committing the expertise of specialist organizers and of officers, and of providing a broader context within which support for workplace activists can be provided. That support can include training, structures linking into the wider decision-making mechanisms within the union, and clear communication of organizing strategy. This coordination of workplace activism is important because it helps us to start to evaluate the wider impact of organizing activity at an aggregate level as well as at the level of individual campaigns. This is the focus of the next chapter.

6

EVALUATING ORGANIZING

Throughout the decade of the development of specialist organizing activity, we have noted a marked change in approach in British unions. The early years of organizing activity prompted many comments and stories from organizers and senior policymakers about the lack of overarching strategic direction to much of the organizing activity taking place. A fairly typical example was a "hot shop" campaign where workers in a call center were dissatisfied about their working conditions (see Simms 2006, 2007b). In brief, the union involved was approached primarily because the husband of one of the most vocal workers was a member, and the organizing department took on the campaign because they were keen to expand into new territory and the call center had links with one of the main employers organized by the union. Although the campaign was successful in gaining recognition for collective bargaining, the long-term sustainability of the campaign was called into question for a number of reasons. First, the union's resources and expertise in supporting members outside the main areas of membership and activism were extremely limited. Second, the union's leverage in the wider labor and service markets within which the targeted employer operated was extremely limited, and this constrained their ability to secure bargaining outcomes. Third, the fact that the workers were outside the core membership meant that they found it difficult to engage in the wider activities of the union, which limited their influence and access to resources to support the union within the workplace. This example illustrates some of the challenges of deciding—and evaluating— the purpose and outcomes of organizing work. It illustrates the need to evaluate a broad range of organizing outcomes. Simply increasing membership, activism, representativeness, and participation does not necessarily ensure sustainable organizing outcomes. In this example, the structure of the union in representing and engaging new membership groups was a barrier to ensuring sustainable success, and the engagement and activism seen during the prerecognition organizing phase of this campaign eventually withered. Arguably, these workers are in a more advantageous position now that they have union bargaining and representation rights, but the hoped for revitalization was not sustained.

However, the example above highlights two importantly different ways of evaluating organizing activity. The first is against the objectives set by the union itself. In the case above, the key objective was to secure collective bargaining rights in this organization. In this regard, the union was remarkably successful. But a broader evaluation must surely ask questions about how the establishment of collective bargaining in this organization strengthens the union in this sector and whether the interests of these members can be promoted more widely within the union and society.

These two ways of evaluating organizing activity are important because if we only take the approach of evaluating outcomes against the objectives unions set themselves, there is a risk that we limit our focus to only the objectives that are considered achievable at that moment in time. Unions are unlikely to set themselves objectives that are perceived to be impossible or even improbable, particularly given that organizing is risky and resource intensive. Thus we take as our starting point the view that the actual objectives set by unions are the outcomes of complex judgments (many of them political) about what is desirable and achievable at that moment. While this tells us a great deal about the contemporary political context (both inside and outside the unions), it risks failing to engage with any broader "vision" of what organizing can and should be about. It is a legitimate criticism (Carter 2006) of some previous evaluation of organizing activity that it has mainly focused on evaluating initiatives against the objectives set by the unions themselves and, thus, risks taking a rather apolitical and ahistorical view of these developments. We therefore take the second approach as well and attempt to evaluate actual organizing outcomes not just against the objectives that were set, but against a wider view of the changes that unions should make in order to (re)establish their roles as strong, independent voices of working people.

This second evaluation is undoubtedly harsher and more contested than the former. But if we do not make any comment on the outcomes of more than a decade of union organizing activity in the United Kingdom as evaluated against some of the wider political objectives, we risk taking a very narrow view both of what organizing is and of what it could achieve. In this chapter, we therefore comment on the evidence of whether or not unions have made progress toward the range of objectives set by the New Unionism project (Heery et al. 2000a) before moving on to consider the wider political agenda underpinning (some) ideas about union organizing. With this distinction in mind, we want to consider the evidence relating to a range of different measures of organizing outcomes: increasing membership, collective bargaining, organizing underrepresented workers, organizing in new sectors, worker self-organization, and union democracy.

Membership

In some respects, the most important outcome of organizing is increasing membership. Undoubtedly part of the rationale for establishing the TUC Organizing Academy, and one of the reasons why we have seen the wider "turn" to organizing, has been the collapse of union membership in the 1980s and 1990s. This is rational and logical; a large proportion of the income of most UK unions depends on membership subscriptions. Declining membership therefore has important negative impact on the income of most unions. Indeed, in the late 1990s, Michael Crosby, then the head of the Australian Congress of Trade Unions (ACTU) Organising Centre, was famous in Australia and the United Kingdom—and probably beyond—for presenting union officers with his "scary graph" that mapped the point at which union income and expenditure crossed and the financial basis of the union became untenable. But the argument is not just one of finances. Without members, unions as collective organizations are largely unsustainable. There are some alternatives—the French model of trade unionism, for example, focuses on recruiting activists rather than "ordinary" members—but these tend to be specific to particular institutional contexts. Australia, the United Kingdom, and the United States all share an important focus on membership recruitment. In these systems, as membership declines, unions lose the legitimacy to speak as the collective voice of workers. Equally, declining membership limits the impact any collective action may have on employers, that is, their coercive power. Declining membership therefore has negative impacts on both the legitimacy power and the coercive power of unions.

Our research shows that individual organizing campaigns are usually very successful in recruiting members. This is not very surprising; organizers are trained to speak to workers and to persuade a considerable proportion of them to join the union. Our early research suggested that academy organizers typically recruited around a thousand members a year; easily enough to pay their salaries. The evidence in relation to individual unions is, however, a little more mixed. We do see evidence of strong membership growth in some unions, and these do tend to be the unions that have recruited organizers and that have been thinking more strategically about how to integrate organizing into the wider work of the union.

But as many people before us have pointed out, membership in individual workplaces or in individual unions is not a sufficient measure of membership strength. Aggregate union membership has stabilized in the United Kingdom during the past ten years. Although most unions would celebrate this as very good news after the hemorrhage of members between 1979 and 1997, there are two very serious notes of concern. First, this stabilization has taken place in a comparatively benign environment. The Labour governments from 1997 to 2010 implemented key policy changes that reinforced the legitimacy of unions. These included setting up a Union Modernization Fund to channel money into efforts by unions to modernize their structures and processes, setting up a Union Learning Fund to encourage unions to promote learning in the workplace, introducing the statutory recognition procedures, and recognizing unions as the legitimate voice of workers on a range of advice bodies such as the Low Pay Commission that recommends the rate of the national minimum wage. Although the Labour governments consistently adopted the view that they would not repeal the restrictions on industrial action that were implemented by the Conservatives in the 1980s and early 1990s, and have not implemented everything that the unions would have liked, the period from 1997 to 2010 was undoubtedly a political and legislative context that was more favorable to unions. It is of concern, therefore, that having invested so much in organizing activity within a benign context, that aggregate union membership has done little more than stabilize. Although it is probably true that membership would have declined further without the investment in organizing, against this background, stabilization is less than optimal.

The second note of concern is that the UK labor force grew significantly from 1997 until the financial crisis of 2008 and recession of 2009. So while absolute levels of membership have stabilized, the number of union members as a proportion of the total labor force (aggregate union density) has continued to decline (Achur 2010, Bryson and Forth 2010). This indicates that the investment in organizing over the past ten years has largely enabled unions to hold steady, rather than to expand into growing sectors of the economy. Much of the employment growth has been through migration, and although there is undoubtedly evidence of innovative practice with some unions taking on the challenge of organizing these workers (Holgate 2009a, 2009b; Simms and Holgate 2010b), evidently there has not been enough of this kind of work to keep pace with the growth in employment. The decline of aggregate union density is of concern because it influences the extent to which both legitimacy and coercive power can be used in collective bargaining and in representing the interests of membership more widely. This is particularly visible in relation to collective bargaining, to which our attention now turns.

Collective Bargaining

Collective bargaining is a good example of how unions can use both legitimacy power and coercive power together. In the context of organizing, unions are typically seeking two related objectives: securing collective bargaining gains at the level of the individual workplace and securing bargaining gains across a sector or subsector of the economy. In a greenfield campaign it is therefore unsurprising that a central objective will usually be to establish collective bargaining in those workplaces, as this gives both legitimacy and a wider range of formal opportunities to use coercive power, because in the UK setting a union has to fulfill a range of legal requirements before it can take industrial action.

At the level of individual campaigns, unions are not as successful as one might expect in securing collective bargaining rights from employers, even with the support of the statutory recognition legislation. It is difficult to give any accurate figures, because it all depends on how we define "a campaign." The start and end points of union organizing campaigns are often very vague, and if workers prove not to be engaging with the union, it is very common that a union will divert resources away from that workplace very quickly. Nonetheless, if we look across the economy, Gall (2007) reports, for example, that there were only 131 cases of both statutory and voluntary recognition granted in 2005, of which 27 were granted through the statutory processes and a further 9 were cases where the statutory processes were used to secure a voluntary deal. What is perhaps more striking about Gall's data is that the number of recognition deals (both voluntary and statutory) being agreed each year has fallen markedly since a peak in 1999, 2000, and 2001. In these years, 365, 525, and 685 deals were made respectively. This almost undoubtedly reflects anticipation of, and then response to, the introduction of the statutory processes. Although the methodologies and time periods vary between Gall's figures and the figures given by the Central Arbitration Committee (CAC) whose job it is to apply and administer the statutory recognition processes, the data trend is very similar. Of course, the CAC only reports on claims taken through the statutory processes, but in the year ending March 2008 there were only 64 applications made. So there is little evidence that the "turn to organizing" in the past decade has radically transformed the patterns of new recognition for collective bargaining in the United Kingdom. In Gall's period of analysis (1995 to 2005) the 2,133 recognition agreements for which he found detailed evidence covered just over 870,000 workers. This was a substantial effort but was not sufficient to expand collective bargaining into new sectors of the economy or to keep up with the pace at which the labor force has expanded during that period.

But organizing in the UK context does not only apply to greenfield sites where recognition is being established. It is therefore useful to look at what has been happening to collective bargaining in areas where unions are already established. Here there is a more positive note. Gall (2007) also highlights the extent to which cases of derecognition have fallen to almost nil since 2000; there have been fewer than 10 cases of derecognition in each year since 2000. Over the time period examined, the 126 cases of derecognition covered only marginally more than 40,000 workers, which does indicate that the union movement has been successful in extending bargaining coverage in absolute terms.

We also need to think about *where* recognition for collective bargaining is being strengthened, and here a very interesting story emerges. Our studies of organizing campaigns are supported by data that focus at an aggregate level, which suggest that unions are relatively cautious about the targeting of their organizing activity. The CAC annual reports consistently show that the sectors that generate the most claims for statutory recognition are the manufacturing, transport, and communication sectors, which have tended to account for well over half and typically nearer three-quarters of applications for statutory recognition. This is supported by academic studies that draw on evidence of recognition agreements from the economy more widely and show that "on the one hand, new recognition agreements are increasing. On the other hand, they are concentrated in places where unions have traditionally been strong and unions are not making much headway in getting into the more dynamic firms that are likely to be the leaders of the future" (Blanden et al. 2006, 186). This relatively bleak picture explains why Gall (2007, 78) characterizes the trend data as "an emerging crisis for trade unions." But he adds a crucial question mark at the end of this summary. Although undoubtedly the aggregate story is one of unions being relatively cautious in their targeting of organizing activity, and in particular focusing on campaigns in sectors where there is already some union presence, it could be argued that this is a logical strategy in relation to consolidating collective bargaining strength.

In our detailed qualitative analysis of five greenfield campaigns that were successful in securing a union presence in the workplace (Simms 2005), we saw clear evidence of the difficulties presented to unions when they gain bargaining rights in a workplace where they have little or no presence in the rest of the sector. These problems include having little experience of the issues and pressures within the sector; having few levers to use in bargaining because competitor employers do not have to deal with unions and are therefore free to set wages, terms, and conditions as they choose; and having a limited ability to demonstrate the effectiveness of collective bargaining because of these difficulties. We know that members and activists are far more likely to walk away from unions they perceive as being ineffective and, predictably, membership and activism collapsed, illustrating the problems of building sustainable unionism when the workplace is so isolated within a nonunionized sector.

It is therefore not so surprising that unions that have sought to expand over the past decade have focused on workplaces in sectors where there is already some bargaining presence. Lerner (cited in Crosby 2005, 743) introduces a further argument as to why this is a desirable approach. He emphasizes that "if only 10 percent of workers in an industry are unionized, it is impossible to have real union democracy because 90 percent of the workers are excluded." In other words, Lerner argues that organizing on an industrial or sectoral level is essential not just to secure bargaining leverage and make an effort to take wages out of competition, but to ensure a democratic representation of workers in that sector. Although the logic of this view is undeniable, some of the consequences are more contested. Crosby's reading of this argument (Crosby 2005) is that this risks overriding the views of members within the union, in favor of attempting to engage workers who are not (yet) members. Crosby argues that Lerner fails to differentiate between workers' control over their jobs (linked to union density) and workers' control over their own organizations (through union elections). He argues that both are centrally important and that "elections matter" (Crosby 2005, 743). We develop our own analysis of this view in our discussion of worker self-organization later in this chapter. But for the moment, it is sufficient to acknowledge that there are important, complex, and contested links between organizing, collective bargaining, and union democracy.

Before we move on to look at other outcomes, we should also note that there is evidence in the United Kingdom that the *scope* of collective bargaining is shrinking considerably. Several important studies (Brown and Nash 2008, Moore and Bewley 2004) have looked at the content of bargaining agreements and concluded that the many collective bargaining rounds cover only "core" issues such as pay, working time, holidays, and training rather than an extended list of issues such as equal opportunities, training, or pensions. This seems to suggest that unions are not succeeding in expanding the scope of joint regulation as an outcome of organizing efforts.

As mentioned earlier, this is of very serious concern when we are seeking to evaluate organizing outcomes against both the objectives that unions set themselves, and any wider view of what organizing might seek to achieve.

In short, these findings signal a potentially very serious problem with the separation of organizing and bargaining. Because most unions have separated negotiating and organizing within their structures, we see a problem in securing bargaining outcomes as a result of investing in organizing activity. Although we are not suggesting that collective bargaining is the be all and end all of trade unionism or of organizing work, it is—and always has been—a central pillar of union activity in the United Kingdom. Some unions such as the GMB are increasingly thinking about how to integrate the organizing and bargaining functions. But these efforts at integration are by no means seen across the board, and very serious questions remain about what role organizing—and organizers—are likely to achieve if those efforts are not focused on securing gains from employers.

Targeting Underrepresented Membership Groups

A further element of this argument, frequently presented by those who focus their attention on the importance of unions increasing membership among underrepresented groups, is that organizing activity can and should target the engagement of specific groups of members in democratic structures. This is particularly seen among authors who discuss women's involvement in unions (Colgan and Ledwith 2002b, Greene and Kirton 2003, Kirton and Healy 2004, McBride 2001, Parker and Douglas 2010). Although in the United Kingdom, women workers are proportionately represented among union membership, they are underrepresented in the decision-making structures. Thus there are those who argue that if organizing efforts do not attempt to address inequality, unions are likely to become increasingly irrelevant within contemporary workplaces and labor markets. Other groups such as young workers, and black and minority ethnic workers are underrepresented in both the membership and representative structures of most unions (Holgate 2004a).

The evidence of organizing outcomes around this is very mixed. Although the original objective to target underrepresented groups was never as specific as it might have been, there are two major groups that can be

considered to be underrepresented in UK union membership: those working in sectors and workplaces where unions have traditionally struggled
to organize, and those from minority ethnic groups where representation
within unions has not been representative of the workforce population.
Although these groups need to be dealt with as analytically separate, there
are important overlaps between them. Overall, minority ethnic workers,
for example, are far more likely to be working in private service-sector
workplaces where union representation is low. Thus the issue of underrepresentation is multifaceted and complex. The intention here is to unpick
some of this complexity and evaluate both the strengths and the weaknesses of union activities.

There is only really one group of workers who can be identified in the
empirical evidence as having been targeted for membership specifically because of their worker characteristics: migrant workers. Other groups have
largely been dealt with as integral to the workplaces selected by unions
for organizing activity. Why this group has been dealt with separately
is open to question. We suspect it reflects the fact that migrant workers
have grown considerably as a feature of the UK labor market in the period under consideration; largely as a consequence of the expansion of EU
membership to the eight Eastern European countries in 2004, which gives
citizens of those countries the right to travel and (usually) to work in other
EU member states. In other words, this is a reflection of unions responding
to labor market change.

Others have studied this phenomenon in far greater detail than we can
here (see Holgate 2009a and 2011, Martínez Lucio and Perrett 2009, Perrett and Martínez Lucio 2009 for a review of the literature in this area),
but it is notable that some separate organizing activity has been targeted
at this group. Putting to one side examples of organizing campaigns that
have taken place in workplaces or organizations that employ largely migrant workers (see Holgate 2005 for an example), there have also been
examples of campaigns, designed to cross workplaces, employers, and sectors, that have targeted migrant workers with information about working
in the United Kingdom. Examples include the development of migrant
worker branches in the GMB, the development of the Justice for Cleaners
campaign in Unite (Holgate 2009b), and Unionlearn projects structured
around the provision of English for Speakers of Other Languages (ESOL)
classes (Martínez Lucio and Perrett 2009, Martínez Lucio et al. 2007).

Although these are all important examples of activity, we must note that the vast majority of migrant workers work in sectors where formal union representation is absent (Portes and French 2005), and the kinds of campaigns highlighted above are notable for the fact that they are atypical. Thus perhaps the more significant challenge is to expand union representation to those sectors and workplaces, which is our focus in the following section where, unfortunately, the assessment of success is rather pessimistic.

Organizing in Underrepresented Sectors

Data from CAC decisions in relation to the statutory recognition procedures, as well as macro-data (Blanden et al. 2006, Gall 2007) persistently show that unions have mainly targeted workplaces in existing strongholds for greenfield organizing activity. As Blanden et al. (2006, 183) point out, "Although the new recognition agreements have helped 'stop the rot' of secular decline, these firms may not be the ones that can help unions increase aggregate membership substantially." This "consolidation" or "close expansion" activity (Kelly and Heery 1989) is argued to be rational by many union policymakers. Consolidation activity or close expansion typically involves increasing membership density in organizations where unions already have recognition and/or are seeking bargaining rights in organizations that are linked to workplaces where recognition already exists. This has the advantage to unions of maximizing the return on their organizing expenditure. Employer resistance is typically less in workplaces where there is already a working relationship. And some unions have invested in expanding recognition agreements to groups of workers in the same organizations, but who have not previously been covered by collective agreements.

There are some examples of particularly innovative practice. The Unite approach discussed in chapter 3 is a good example. There are also examples of some of the smaller, cash-rich unions seeking to expand. Specifically the Iron and Steel Trades Confederation (ISTC) and Graphic, Paper, and Media Union (GPMU), which had strongholds in the declining steel and paper industries respectively, were early supporters of the academy. They developed slightly different approaches. The ISTC adopted what they called "community unionism" and sought to organize in the sectors where ex-steelworkers and their families now worked. They argued their stronghold was in communities that had developed to provide labor for steel plants, and now that those plants no longer hired large numbers of workers, the union should seek to recruit and organize in the often service-based workplaces that had taken their place. In 2004, the union merged with several smaller unions and calls itself Community to reflect this strategy and these values. However, in 2010, the union disbanded its organizing unit reflecting a significant shift of strategy within the union and debates about the extent to which this type of organizing activity had been effective in providing opportunities for renewal.

The GPMU took a similar approach in response to declining employment in the printing industry, but it was more successfully able to use the statutory recognition legislation, because although there had been a wave of derecognition efforts in printing throughout the 1980s and 1990s, many workers had retained either membership or an affiliation to the union despite not having bargaining rights. In practice, this meant that there were pockets of considerable membership density where majority support for the union was comparatively easy to demonstrate, but where employer hostility to union recognition had blocked bargaining for many years. Alongside this approach, the GPMU did attempt to expand beyond printing. This work was largely undertaken by academy organizers and involved targeting workforces working in similar geographical locations to members in existing firms; for example, workplaces on an industrial estate near a small print shop. Again, this strategy yielded some membership expansion but little overall membership growth. The union eventually merged with Amicus (later Unite) in 2004.

These examples are also notable because they are atypical. The main picture of union organizing activity over the past decade has been one of consolidation and close expansion rather than expansion into new sectors. Most notably, overall, there has been very little evidence at an aggregate level of expansion into the private service sector. Membership density in the private service sector still hovers around 15.5 percent, reflecting a steady downward trend from around 20 percent in 1997 (Forth and Bryson 2010). Of course, there is also a significant public-sector effect here. Public-sector unions make up a large proportion of the Organising Academy sponsors, and these unions generally have fewer opportunities to expand their recognition agreements as most public-sector workers have union representation rights. Thus for these unions it seems obvious that consolidation is the main organizing activity that they undertake. However, the public sector has been increasingly privatized over recent decades, and it is not unusual for a local Unison branch to have up to two hundred employers in its area where it would in the past only have had one local authority employer.

The Public and Commercial Services Union (PCS) also has had large numbers of members transferred to the private sector as a result of privatization polices of successive governments during the past twenty years. Many of these members have taken with them their union representation rights as a result of complex European Union legislation that, in principle, protects some of these workers' terms and conditions as they are transferred to the private sector (McMullen 2006). This has given PCS a foothold in many private-sector organizations that had largely not been unionized. While efforts to capitalize on these organizing opportunities have had mixed outcomes, they do at least represent an opportunity—and in many respects a necessity—for some public-sector unions to expand into new territories.

In short, while there is evidence that some unions have been seeking to expand into new territories, this is not the only picture. Overall, collective bargaining coverage is now around 32 percent of workers compared to 36 percent in 1999, reflecting a slight downward trend in both public and private sectors (Forth and Bryson 2010). It is therefore hard to avoid the conclusion that thirteen years of organizing activity has made comparatively little impact on formal, aggregate measures of union power. Of course, it is impossible to know whether decline would have been worse in the absence of such activity. We strongly suspect it would have been and that much of the stabilization of union membership has resulted from the kinds of activities described throughout the book. But on these measures there is comparatively little cause for celebration within the union movement as the United Kingdom moves into a period that is likely to be both significantly more challenging politically and economically than the previous thirteen years. But as anyone who has ever discussed organizing with a union organizer will know, organizing is not just about numbers. It is also about building strong and (relatively) independent structures of worker representation. We feel that it is important to try to capture this kind of "cultural" development in our evaluation and, despite the methodological difficulties of evaluating something that is inherently difficult to measure, we feel that our data allow us important insight into the extent to which the UK union movement has developed ideas about worker self-organization, union democracy, and how to make links beyond the workplace. It is to this that our attention now turns.

Worker Self-Organization and Union Democracy

One of the central notions within organizing is that it should encourage membership activism so that workers develop the confidence to take collective action to address their own problems and issues at work. Through collective action around relevant workplace issues, it is then hoped that workers will come to experience the effectiveness of collective action and join the union. This "mobilization" approach (Kelly 1998) places at its core workers taking responsibility for addressing their workplace issues, rather than relying on paid officers. As a result, it raises some crucial issues about ideas of union democracy. Union democracy is a highly contested notion. In previous chapters, we have already raised the question of whether union democracy relates to the processes through which members participate in their union, or whether we should take a broader view of what would traditionally have been called "industrial democracy," in other words, the need to engage workers in the decision making of their employers at both organizational and industrial or sectoral levels.

We take the view that while both are important objectives of organizing, "industrial democracy" in the UK context is largely secured through collective bargaining, which has been discussed previously. Unlike, for example, Germany, we have weak institutional mechanisms for industrial democracy to extend beyond collective bargaining (Hall et al. 2009), and they are unlikely to strengthen in the foreseeable future. As a result, we suggest that arguments about what institutional or legislative frameworks for wider industrial democracy may or may not be desirable are beyond the scope of this book. If organizing efforts were sufficiently successful to (re)establish unions as powerful actors within the economic and political environment such debates would not only be logical, but essential. But at this point, we want to focus on the internal mechanisms available to members to participate in their unions. In doing so, we differentiate between participation at the workplace level and participation in the wider structures of the union.

It is difficult to get aggregate-level evidence about what is happening in organizing campaigns in individual workplaces, but we can make some helpful inferences from our in-depth qualitative case studies of campaigns. Although these are mostly greenfield campaigns, we nonetheless get important insight, which indicates significant variability both within and between campaigns. Variation within a campaign tends to be related to the individual activists in particular workplaces, and this is where activist training becomes so important. It is important to note that there are increasing opportunities for activists to be trained in organizing techniques and principles. But until relatively recently, activist training in most unions had—at best—a single module on organizing, which rather undermined much of the good work done during organizing campaigns and undoubtedly sent very mixed messages about what role(s) unions want their activists to take on. In 2009, the TUC launched the Activist Academy which is certainly a positive development in this area, and many individual unions are giving serious thought and resources to ways of developing activists more effectively.

Variation between campaigns is largely related to the policies and practices of individual unions, and this is perhaps conceptually one of the most interesting issues emerging from our extensive studies of organizing activity. In the earlier section on collective bargaining, we highlighted the difficulties confronting unions if they pay insufficient attention to the link between organizing and bargaining. There is a serious danger that uncoordinated organizing activity results in individual workplaces being organized, but with little opportunity to secure effective collective bargaining gains because of the lack of unionization in the wider industry or sector. But we also argue that the reverse is equally problematic. Organizing that is driven too much from the top or from the center of the union can be just as unsustainable.

We see this in a number of campaigns that have been launched because—and only because—they have been strategically important to the union for some reason. Typically, this might be because of some kind of change of ownership (for example, if an employer subcontracts or outsources a particular activity, which transfers some union members into another employer) or because a union is seeking to expand beyond its core territories.

Although both kinds of organizing are necessary, there are examples of campaigns that have been pursued even where there is little enthusiasm from workers. Because of the voluntarist nature of British labor relations, it is quite possible that managers may agree to a union presence, or even to collective bargaining, without a strong demand for it from workers. Thus we have seen cases where unions pursue some of these campaigns and attempt to build membership and activism, but where the membership withers quickly. We argue that this kind of organizing is equally as unsustainable as campaigns where there is membership enthusiasm, but where there is a lack of coordination.

Which returns us to important ideas about union democracy. Much previous writing on union democracy tends to focus on membership activism. Indeed Fairbrother (1989, 2000a), for example, argues that workplace activism is the key driver of both organizing and of union renewal more widely, and Bramble (1995) argues that efforts at coordination are "stifling" renewal opportunities. On the basis of having observed many campaigns, we take a different view. In common with Voss and Sherman (2000) we argue that organizing activity is an area that needs coordination if it is to succeed in developing sustainable and effective trade unionism. This is explicitly not the same as arguing that organizing strategy should be driven from "top down" or "center out." Crucially, we see the role of the "top" or the "center" as being one of coordination and allocation of scarce resources, rather than of control over what happens in the workplace itself. We also argue that, within the UK context, organizing is achieving little without developing strong workplace activism and membership. We are not arguing that this coordinated approach produces no tensions. Clearly, any process of allocating scarce resources can create tension, and we have highlighted these throughout this book. Rather, our argument rests on an analysis of the conditions under which the most effective organizing outcomes emerge, and in our view, our data clearly show a role for both activism and coordination.

This highlights the paradox of organizing; there is almost no evidence that organizing activity is currently happening spontaneously within UK workplaces so it must be promoted by professional union actors (officials, organizers, policymakers). But if those professionals do manage to create effectively organized workplaces, ultimately, these two loci of activity may well come into conflict with each other. And this is where the structures of union democracy, that is, the internal decision-making structures of the union, are so important. If centrally coordinated organizing efforts are successful in creating dynamic workplace organization this should be seen in workplaces that have high levels of membership, members who participate in the activities of the union (including, but not limited to, bargaining), membership that is representative of the workforce in those workplaces, and—and this is hugely important—the confidence to set a union agenda that is relevant in that workplace. The first three of these objectives are rarely contested by either workplace activists or by union professionals. The latter, which we consider to be a central part of any consideration of any meaningful definition of worker self-organization, is highly contested.

Indeed, it is this point that is really the key difference between the different approaches of unions that we have described elsewhere (see Simms and Holgate 2010b for an initial discussion). Many trade unionists, commentators, and academics are very critical of the kind of organizing undertaken by, for example, USDAW. We use USDAW as an example here because we have described their approach in more detail than many other unions, and also because they are very clear that a key focus of their organizing activity is about recruitment, not because we think their approach is any more problematic than many other unions with which we have worked. USDAW's approach fully accepts the importance of increasing membership, of ensuring representativeness, and of developing activists. However, the structure and culture of USDAW places far less emphasis on building worker self-organization. In part, this is because of the labor markets within which USDAW organizes. Within retail, workers often work on temporary and/or part-time contracts, and labor turnover is high, which can make these workplaces difficult to organize. USDAW has taken the view that one way around these challenges is to work with employer support wherever possible. And the politics of that approach cannot be ignored. One consequence of a more "partnership"-oriented approach is that it leaves less scope for members to build a workplace trade union culture that develops a collective and independent voice around relevant workplace issues than in unions that place less emphasis on working cooperatively with employers. So, although USDAW has undoubtedly been successful in recruiting members and growing the union, and has had some considerable success in identifying workplace activists, there is little emphasis on building worker self-organization. It should be noted that many within the union would argue that this is neither a desirable nor an achievable objective, and it doesn't therefore matter whether one rejects it because of a political stance, or because of an acceptance that it would be difficult to achieve organizing in these sectors; the end result is the same.

Inevitably, however, unions that do seek to develop strong, self-organizing workplaces are highly likely to find tensions between the central coordination of union activities (including organizing) and the aspiration to involve members at workplace level so that they make decisions that are relevant to them. This is a further paradox inherent within organizing. But we argue that it is a paradox that has always been inherent within trade unionism more generally and is not specific to organizing activity. What is different is that some ideas about organizing—although not all as we can see from the USDAW example above—relate either explicitly or implicitly to an objective of increasing the democratic participation of members.

In practice, most unions—and certainly most organizers—are committed to the objective of increasing the democratic participation of members. And where organizing campaigns are successful in increasing membership and representation structures there are relatively few examples of efforts to control members in a direct manner. Indeed, in some respects our findings show that it can be officers and organizers who are disappointed by the fact that members seem unenthused about participating in the workplace structures. One officer of a large union that had run both greenfield and in-fill campaigns in large private-sector companies stressed at length how hard she tried to encourage members to take on representation and bargaining roles—not always successfully: "My approach is that they [workplace activists] should be doing this kind of thing for themselves." She went on to say, "I think they [activists] should have the responsibility for it [the campaign]. It's their workplace, their problems, not mine."

This is a fairly typical view of many officers and of almost all organizers. Indeed, while it is undoubtedly the case that not all union officers share this view, we have yet to come across an organizer who does not broadly share this approach. Where officers do not share this view, it can lead to tensions. Focusing for the moment on campaigns where officers and organizers do share this approach, it is clear even in those campaigns that there can be frustrations about getting workplace activists to take on these roles.

This is particularly evident in greenfield campaigns where workers often have little previous experience of unions. In some respects this can be an advantage in that their expectations can be shaped throughout the campaigns. But in practice these new union members, activists, and representatives often need time and training to build and develop experience and confidence. A further complication is that in greenfield campaigns, our research shows that the range of activities taken on by activists can be very different from the roles adopted once recognition has been granted and the union is more established. These different roles demand different skills and require, we argue, acceptance of the fact that the pre- and postrecognition phases of greenfield organizing are very different, requiring different skills, and sometimes different activists.

The postrecognition phase is essentially an in-fill campaign. In-fill campaigns are where issues of the relationship between union organizing and union democracy really come to the fore. Here, activists and representatives often have a great deal of experience within their unions, and can often have very strong ideas about how they envisage the relationship and the division of decision-making responsibilities between officers and activists.

Although there can be tensions around this, unions have well-established structures for engaging members and activists, which channel those debates into conferences and other decision-making processes. This is how unions operate, and it is what they do—and always have done. There seems little evidence that organizing per se presents a serious challenge to those existing processes and structures. Indeed many officers and organizers would like to see greater involvement of members, even if the consequence was to make their role more contested.

Social Movement Unionism

Some authors and commentators have seen the opportunity to broaden debates about organizing to include ideas about the focus of unions more generally. One important strand of this has been an increasingly strong view that unions can and should develop a form of "social movement unionism" (Clawson 2003). Typically this tends to focus on developing formal and informal links between unions and other social justice campaigns to improve workers' rights. This implicitly accepts a more radical view of the role unions can play in social change and promoting social justice that may conflict with some of the more institutional and regulationist objectives discussed above. In the United Kingdom, there is relatively little evidence of this kind of organizing, although this view has been most closely associated with "community unionism" (Holgate 2009c, McBride and Greenwood 2009, Wills and Simms 2004), which focuses on increasing the links between the workplace and the wider community, and on recognizing and building on workers' roles and connections beyond their workplace. What is important here is that the focus of such organizing activity is far beyond any immediate improvements in workers' terms and conditions (although these may accrue from such activity), and that the union attempts to become relevant to workers' lives beyond a workplace, industry, or sectoral level. Social movement unionism has a far broader view of the role of the union, taking it beyond the workplace and into the wider political sphere.

And, again, we need to be alert to the different national contexts. Unions in the United Kingdom have a long history of taking up broadly defined social justice campaigns and issues, including antiracism campaigns, concern with local development issues, and an extremely active engagement in the "learning agenda" focused on improving basic skills such as literacy and numeracy among workers. But the focus on collective bargaining, the separation of the Labour Party and the trade union movement, and the dominance of the idea of incremental rather than revolutionary change help to explain why UK unions have tended to prioritize workplace bargaining over wider community activity.

Our research indicates that the interest and investment in organizing activity is still located very much at workplace level and prioritizes the objective of securing improvements in workers' terms and conditions of employment. This is not the same as saying that unions have no interest in the wider social movement agenda; rather that it is not their central priority. We argue that this does reflect a certain lack of imagination on behalf of unions. Elsewhere, it has been argued that certain labor market conditions such as the employment of large numbers of contingent workers could give unions a reason to organize "beyond the enterprise" (Heery et al. 2004). We do see evidence that particular labor markets can create this kind of union response, and there are certainly examples of unions organizing freelance and self-employed workers in this way. But this is by no means the dominant form of union organizing in the United Kingdom.

Conclusions

In a broad sense, the evidence of the impact of organizing initiatives is very mixed and presents few reasons for optimism regarding wide-scale union renewal. In large part, we have argued that this is a consequence of the dominant focus of organizing practice targeted at membership development and, occasionally, securing recognition for collective bargaining rather than the wider and more political objectives of promoting worker self-organization or social movement unionism.

Our analysis has allowed a more complex evaluation of the dynamics of particular outcomes in different unions and different sectors than has previously been put forward in much of the UK literature. This has allowed us to develop a more nuanced argument than has been outlined in previous literature and one that can more convincingly account for the diversity of objectives and outcomes identified across the union movement. We argue that while at a general level, there has been an interest in increasing membership at the expense of a more radical "vision" of organizing, there are notable exceptions that have placed considerable emphasis on strengthening membership voice and activism.

Overall though, our analysis has a decidedly pessimistic tone. Returning to the relevance of the wider political and economic context of the period between 1997 and 2010, it is clear that unions largely failed to use the more benign environment to renew themselves in a convincing manner. Although membership levels have stabilized, this is against a background of a growing labor market. Although there are examples of innovative projects to attract new and underrepresented groups of vulnerable workers (such as migrant workers), there is considerable evidence that collective bargaining strength during this period has declined in almost all sectors. Equally, there is little evidence of any sustained development of the kind of social movement unionism discussed in US literature. On all of these measures, the UK union movement is judged to be at least no stronger—and probably weaker—than it was in 1997 despite the changes in the institutional and political context.

Clearly the economic and political contexts in the United Kingdom have shifted rapidly since the financial crisis of 2008. The 2010 center-Right UK coalition government has proved largely uninterested in worker and union rights, although they have hinted that if social unrest were to become more evident, the may seek to tighten further the restrictions on industrial action. In common with much of the European Union, the United Kingdom faces an extended period of economic austerity. The effects of these external factors on unions and on the organizing project remain to be seen. But it is evident that we face a challenging period ahead.

We leave the final word with one of our most senior interviewees whose role is to develop and deliver strategic leadership across the UK union movement. She stressed the need for unions to keep organizing in the current climate.

> Globally, labor's share of wealth decreases. Globally the neoliberal cult makes it hard to restrain union-free capital. International policies make it hard in a central way. These are big, big issues. Not just for the trade union movement, but for progressives globally about how do you keep going when it feels like things are stacked against you. . . . It probably means that we need to think even more internationally than we've ever thought before. We need to think longer term than we've thought before, in say not just next year, or five years even. But ten years, twenty years, fifty years where will the trade union movement be? What do we need to have done? We need to be savvy politically. (Interviewee #15, white female)

Bibliography

Achur, James. 2010. *Trade Union Membership 2009.* London: Department of Business, Enterprise and Regulatory Reform and National Statistics.

Autor, David H., Frank Levy, and Richard J. Murnane. 2003. "The Skill Content of Recent Technical Change: An Empirical Investigation." *Quarterly Journal of Economics* 118(4): 1279–1333.

Bacon, Nicholas, and Peter Samuel. 2009. "Partnership Agreement Adoption and Survival in the British Private and Public Sectors." *Work, Employment, and Society* 23(2): 231–248.

Badigannavar, Vidu, and John Kelly. 2011. "Partnership and Organizing: An Empirical Assessment of Two Contrasting Approaches to Union Revitalization in the UK." *Economic and Industrial Democracy* 32(1): 5–27.

Bain, George Sayers, and Farouk Elsheikh. 1976. *Union Growth and the Business Cycle.* Oxford: Blackwell.

Bain, George Sayers, and Robert J. Price. 1980. *Profiles of Union Growth: A Comparative Statistical Portrait of Eight Countries.* Oxford: Blackwell.

Banks, Andy. 1991. "The Power and Promise of Community Unionism." *Labor Research Review* 10 (fall/winter): 17–31.

Batstone, Eric, Ian Boraston, and Stephen Frenkel. 1977. *Shop Stewards in Action.* Oxford: Blackwell.

Black Trade Union Solidarity Movement (BTUSM). 1983. *Black Trade Union Solidarity Movement Newsletter.* London.

Blanchflower, David G., and Alex Bryson. 2004. *The Union Wage Premium in the US and the UK.* CEPDP, 612. London: Centre for Economic Performance, London School of Economics and Political Science.

Blanden, Jo, Stephen Machin, and John van Reeven. 2006. "Have Unions Turned a Corner? New Evidence on Recent Trends in Union Recognition in UK Firms." *British Journal of Industrial Relations* 44(2): 169–190.

Blyton, Paul, and Peter Turnbull. 2004. *The Dynamics of Employee Relations.* Basingstoke: Palgrave MacMillan.

Bradley, Harriet, Geraldine Healy, and Nupur Mukerjee. 2002a. *A Double Disadvantage? Minority Ethnic Women in Trade Unions.* ESRC: Future of Work Programme.

———. 2002b. *Inclusion, Exclusion, and Separate Organisation—Black Women Activists in Trade Unions.* ESRC Working Paper 25, Swindon.

Bramble, Tom. 1995. "Deterring Democracy? Australia's New Generation of Trade Union Officials." *Journal of Industrial Relations* (September): 401–426.

Bronfenbrenner, Kate. 1994. Winning against the Odds: Successful Union Strategies for Winning NLRB Certification Elections. Working paper. Cornell University.

Bronfenbrenner, Kate, Sheldon Friedman, Richard W. Hurd, Rudolph A. Oswald, and Ronald L. Seeber, eds. 1998. *Organizing to Win: New Research on Union Strategies.* Ithaca: Cornell University Press.

Bronfenbrenner, Kate, and Robert Hickey. 2004. "Changing to Organize: A National Assessment of Union Strategies." In *Rebuilding Labor: Organizing and Organizers in the New Union Movement,* edited by Ruth Milkman and Kim Voss, 17–61. Ithaca: Cornell University Press.

Bronfenbrenner, Kate, and Tom Juravich. 1998. "It Takes More Than House Calls: Organising To Win with a Comprehensive Union-Building Strategy." In *Organizing to Win: New Research on Union Strategies,* edited by Kate Bronfenbrenner, Sheldon Friedman, Richard W. Hurd, Rudolph A. Oswald, and Ronald L. Seeber, 19–36. Ithaca: Cornell University Press.

Brown, William, and David Nash. 2008. "What Has Been Happening to Collective Bargaining Under New Labour? Interpreting WERS 2004." *Industrial Relations Journal* 39(2): 91–103.

Bryson, Alex, and John Forth. 2010. *Trade Union Membership and Influence, 1999–2009.* London: NIESR Discussion Paper No. 362.

Bryson, Alex, and Rafael Gomez. 2005. "Why Have Workers Stopped Joining Unions? The Rise in Never Membership in Britain." *British Journal of Industrial Relations* 43(1): 67–92.

Buechler, Steven, and F. Kurt Cylke Jr. 1997. *Social Movements: Perspectives and Issues.* California: Mayfield.

Carter, Bob. 2000. "Adoption of the Organising Model in British Trade Unions: Some Evidence from Manufacturing, Science, and Finance." *Work, Employment, and Society* 14(1): 117–136.

———. 2006. "Trade Union Organizing and Renewal: A Response to de Turbeville." *Work, Employment, and Society* 20(2): 415–426.

Carter, Bob, and Peter Fairbrother. 1998. "Coherence or Contradiction? The TUCs New Unionism Project." Paper presented at the Work Employment & Society Conference, 14–16 September 1998, University of Cambridge.

Chamberlayne, Prue, Joanna Bornat, and Tom Wengraf. 2000. "The Biographical Turn." In *The Turn to Biographical Method in Social Science: Comparative Issues and Examples,* edited by Prue Chamberlayne, Joanna Bornat, and Tom Wengraf, 1–31. London: Routleldge.

Clawson, Dan. 2003. *The Next Upsurge: Labor and the New Social Movements.* Ithaca: Cornell University Press.

Cobble, Dorothy Sue. 1993. "Remaking Unions for the New Majority." In *Women and Unions,* edited by Dorothy Sue Cobble, 3–24. Ithaca: Cornell University Press.

Cockburn, Cynthia. 1991. *In the Way of Women: Men's Resistance to Sex Equality in Organizations.* Ithaca: ILR Press.

Colgan, Fiona, and Sue Ledwith. 2002a. "Gender and Diversity: Reshaping Union Democracy." *Employee Relations* 24(2): 167–189.

———. 2002b. *Gender, Diversity, and Trade Unions.* London: Routledge.

Colling, Trevor, and Linda Dickens. 2001. "Gender Equality and the Trade Unions: A New Basis for Mobilization?" In *Equality, Diversity, and Disadvantage in Employment,* edited by Mike Noon and Emmanuel Ogbonna, 136–155. Basingstoke: Palgrave.

Commission on Industrial Relations (CIR). 1974. Mansfield Hosiery Mills. Commission on Industrial Relations Paper No. 76. London: Her Majesty's Stationary Office (HMSO).

Commission for Racial Equality (CRE). 1985. *Trade Union Structures and Black Workers' Participation: A Study in Central Lancashire.* London: Commission for Racial Equality.

Conley, Hazel. 2005. "Front Line or All Fronts? Women's Trade Union Activism in Retail Services." *Gender, Work, and Organization* 12(5): 479–496.

Cooper, Rae. 2000. "Organise, Organise, Organise! ACTU Congress 2000." *Journal of Industrial Relations* 42(4): 582–594.

Craft, James, and Marian Extejt. 1983. "New Strategies in Union Organizing." *Journal of Labor Research* 4(1): 20–32.

Crompton, Rosemary. 2008. *Class and Stratification.* Polity Press: Cambridge, UK

Crosby, Jeff. 2005. "Democracy, Density, and Transformation: We Need Them All." *Working USA.* 8 (December): 733–753.

Darlington, Ralph. 2010. "The State of Workplace Union Reps' Organisation in Britain Today." *Capital and Class* 34(1): 126–135.

Delbridge, Rick. 1998. *Life on the Line in Contemporary Manufacturing.* Oxford: Oxford University Press.

de Turberville, Simon. 2004. "Does the 'Organizing Model' Represent a Credible Union Renewal Strategy?" *Work, Employment, and Society* 18(4): 775–794.

Dickens, Linda, and Mark Hall. 2006. "Fairness—Up to a Point: Assessing the Impact of New Labour's Employment Legislation." *Human Resource Management Journal* 16(4): 338–356.

DiMaggio, Paul J., and Walter W. Powell. 1983. "The Iron Cage Revisited: Institutional Isomorphism and Collective Rationality in Organizational Fields." *American Sociological Review* 48(2): 147–160

Disney, Richard. 1990. "Explanations of the Decline in Trade Union Density in Britain: An Appraisal." *British Journal of Industrial Relations* 28(2): 165–177.

Dølvik, Jon E., and Jeremy Waddington. 2004. "Organizing Marketized Services: Are Trade Unions Up to the Job?" *Economic and Industrial Democracy* 25(1): 9–40.

Donovan Commission. 1968. *Royal Commission on Trade Unions and Employers' Associations.* London: HMSO.

Dunn, B. 2010. "Labour and Community or Labour as Community: (Re-)conceiving the Causes of Decline and Strategies for Renewal." *Work, Employment, and Society Conference.* University of Brighton, September 7–9th.

Edwards, Paul K. 2003. "The Employment Relationship and the Field of Industrial Relations." In *Industrial Relations: Theory and Practice,* edited by Paul K. Edwards, 1–36. Oxford: Blackwells.

Fairbrother, Peter. 1989. *Workplace Unionism in the 1980s: A Process of Renewal.* London: Workers Educational Association.

———. 1996. "Workplace Trade Unionism in the State Sector." In *The New Workplace and Trade Unionism,* edited by Peter Ackers, Chris Smith, and Paul Smith, 110–148. London: Routledge.

———. 2000a. "British Trade Unions Facing the Future." *Capital and Class* 24(2) (summer): 11–42.

———. 2000b. *Unions at the Crossroads.* London: Mansell.

Fantasia, Richard. 1988. *Cultures of Solidarity: Consciousness, Action, and Contemporary American Workers.* Berkeley: University of California Press.

Findlay, Patricia, and Alan McKinlay. 2003. "Union Organising in 'Big Blue's' Backyard." *Industrial Relations Journal* 34(1): 52–66.

Fiorito, Jack, Paul Jarley, and John T. Delaney. 1995. "National Union Effectiveness in Organizing: Measures and Influences." *Industrial and Labor Relations Review* 48: 613–635.

Foerster, Amy. 2003. "Labor's Youth Brigade: What Can the Organizing Institute and its Graduates Tell Us about the Future of Organized Labor?" *Labor Studies Journal* 28(3): 1–31.

Forth, John, and Alex Bryson. 2010. *Trade Union Membership and Influence 1999–2009.* NIESR Discussion Paper 362. September 2010. London: National Institute for Economic and Social Research.

Freeman Richard. 1995. "Are Your Wages Set in Bejing?" *Journal of Economic Perspectives* 9(3): 15–32.

Freeman, Richard, and Jeffery Pelletier. 1990. "The Impact of Industrial Relations Legislation on British Union Density." *British Journal of Industrial Relations* 28(2): 141–64.

French, John R. P., and Bertram Raven. 1960. "The Bases of Social Power." In *Group Dynamics,* edited by Dorwin Cartwright and Alvin Zander, 607–623. New York: Harper and Row.

Gall, Gregor. 2004a. "Trade Union Recognition in Britain 1995–2002: Turning a Corner?" *Industrial Relations Journal* 35(3): 249–270.

———. 2004b. "British Employer Resistance to Trade Union Recognition." *Human Resource Management Journal* 14(2): 36–53.

———. 2007. "Trade Union Recognition in Britain: An Emerging Crisis for Trade Unions?" *Economic and Industrial Democracy* 28(1): 78–109.

Gamson, William A. 1995. "Constructing Social Protest." In *Social Movements and Culture,* edited by Hank Johnston and Bert Klandermans, 85–106. Abingdon: Routledge.

Gennard, John. 2002. "Employee Relations Public Policy Developments 1997–2001: A Break with the Past." *Employee Relations* 24(6): 581–594.

Goos, Maarten, and Alan Manning. 2007. "Lousy and Lovely Jobs: Polarization of Work in Britain." *Review of Economics and Statistics* 89(1): 118–133.

Grabelsky, Jeffrey, and Richard Hurd. 1994. "Reinventing the Organizing Union: Strategies for Change." In *Proceedings of the 46th Annual Meeting of the Industrial Relations Association,* edited by Paula Voos, 84–95. Madison: Industrial Relations Research Association.

Greene, Anne-Marie, and Gill Kirton. 2003. "Advancing Gender Equality: The Role of Women-Only Trade Union Education." *Gender, Work, and Organization* 9(1): 39–59.

Hall, Mark, Sue Hutchinson, John Purcell, Michael Terry, and Jane Parker. 2009. *Implementing Information and Consulation: Evidence from Longitudinal Case Studies in Organisations with 150 or More Employees.* Employment Relations Research Series No. 150. London: Department for Business, Innovation and Skills.

Healy, Geraldine, Harriet Bradley, and Nupur Mukerjee. 2004a. "Individualism and Collectivism Revisited: A Study of Black and Minority Ethnic Women." *Industrial Relations Journal* 35(5): 451–466.

Healy, Geraldine, Edmund Heery, Phil Taylor, and William Brown. 2004b. *The Future of Worker Representation.* London: Palgrave.

Heery, Edmund. 1998a. "The Relaunch of the Trades Union Congress." *British Journal of Industrial Relations* 36(3): 339–360.

———. 1998b. "Campaigning for Part-Time Workers." *Work, Employment, and Society* 12: 351–366.

———. 2002. "Partnership versus Organising: Alternative Futures for British Trade Unionism." *Industrial Relations Journal* 33(1): 20–35.

———. 2003. "Trade Unions and Industrial Relations." In *Understanding Work and Employment: Industrial Relations in Transition* edited by Peter Ackers and Adrian Wilkinson, 278–304. Oxford: Oxford University Press.

———. 2004. "The Trade Union Response to Agency Labour in Britain." *Industrial Relations Journal* 35(5): 434–450.

Heery, Edmund, Hazel Conley, Rick Delbridge, and Paul Stewart. 2004. "Beyond the Enterprise: Trade Union Representation of Freelancers in the UK." *Human Resource Management Journal* 14(2): 20–35.

Heery, Edmund, Rick Delbridge, Melanie Simms, John Salmon and David H. Simpson. 2003. "Organising for Renewal: A Case Study of the TUC's Organising Academy." In *Labor Revitalization: Global Perspectives and New Initiatives,* edited by Dan Cornfield and Holly McCammon, 79–110. New York: JAI Press.

Heery, Edmund, and John Kelly. 1988. "Do Female Representatives Make a Difference? Women Full-Time Officials and Trade Union Work." *Work, Employment, and Society* 2: 487–505.

Heery, Edmund, John Kelly, and Jeremy Waddington. 2003. "Union Revitalization in Britain." *European Journal of Industrial Relations* 9: 79–97.

Heery, Edmund, and Melanie Simms. 2008. "Constraints on Union Organising in the United Kingdom." *Industrial Relations Journal* 39(1): 24–42.

Heery, Edmund, Melanie Simms, Rick Delbridge, John Salmon, and David Simpson. 2000a. "Union Organizing in Britain: A Survey of Policy and Practice." *International Journal of Human Resource Management* 11(5): 986–1007.

———. 2000b. "The TUCs Organising Academy: An Assessment." *Industrial Relations Journal* 31(5): 400–415.

———. 2003a. "Trade Union Recruitment Policy in Britain: Form and Effects." In *Union Organizing. Campaigning for Trade Union Recognition,* edited by Gregor Gall, 56–78. London: Routledge.

Heery, Edmund, Melanie Simms, Dave Simpson, Rick Delbridge, and John Salmon. 2000. "Organizing Unionism Comes to the UK." *Employee Relations* 22(1): 38–57.

Hochschild, Arlie Russell, and Anne Machung. 1989. *The Second Shift: Working Parents and the Revolution at Home.* New York: Viking-Penguin.

Holgate, Jane. 2004a. *Black and Minority Ethnic Worker and Trade Unions: Strategies for Organisation, Recruitment, and Inclusion.* London: Trades Union Congress.

———. 2004b. "Organising Black and Minority Ethnic Workers: Trade Union Strategies for Recruitment and Inclusion." Ph.D. diss., University of London.

———. 2005. "Organising Migrant Workers: A Case Study of Working Conditions and Unionisation at a Sandwich Factory in London." *Work, Employment, and Society* 19(3): 463–480.

———. 2009a. *The Role of UK Unions in the Civic Integration of Immigrant Workers.* Labor Unions and Civic Integration of Immigrant Workers Research Project.

———. 2009b. *Unionising the Low Paid in London: The Justice for Cleaners Campaign.* Case study. Labor Unions and Civic Integration of Immigrant Workers Research Project.

———. 2009c. "Contested Terrain: London's Living Wage Campaign and the Tension between Community and Union Organising." In *The Complexity of Community Unionism: a Comparative Analysis of Concepts and Contexts,* edited by Jo McBride and Ian Greenwood, 49–74. Basingstoke: Palgrave Macmillan.

———. 2011. "Temporary Migrant Workers and Labor Organization." *WorkingUSA* 14: 191–199.

Holgate, Jane, and Melanie Simms. 2008. *10 Years of the Organising Academy.* TUC New Unionism pamphlet series. London: TUC.

Holgate, Jane, and Jane Wills. 2007. "Organising Labor in London: Lessons from the Living Wage Campaign." In *Labor in the New Urban Battlefields: Local Solidarity in a Global Economy,* edited by Lowell Turner and Dan Cornfield, 211–223. Ithaca: Cornell University Press.

Humphrey, Jill C. 2002. *Towards a Politics of the Rainbow: Self-Organization in the Trade Union Movement.* Aldershot: Ashgate.

Hurd, Richard. 1993. "Organizing and Representing Clerical Workers: The Harvard Model." In *Women and Unions: Forging a Partnership,* edited by Dorothy Sue Cobble, 316–336. Ithaca: Cornell University Press.

———. 1998. "Contesting the Dinosaur Image: The Labor Movement's Search for a Future." *Labor Studies Journal* 22: 5–30.

Hyman, Richard. 1997. "The Future of Employee Representation." *British Journal of Industrial Relations* 35(3): 309–336.

————. 1999. "Imagined Solidarities: Can Trade Unions Resist Globalisation?" In *Globalization and Labour Relations,* edited by Peter Leisink, 94–115. Cheltenham: Edward Elgar.

Jarley, Paul. 2001. "Managed Activism: Rationalization, Innovation, and the Organizing Model in Local Unions." Unpublished paper.

Jenkins, Jean. 2007. "Gambling Partners? The Risky Outcomes of Workplace Partnerships." *Work, Employment, and Society* 21(4): 635–652.

Lerner, Stephen. 1992. "Let's Get Moving! Labor's Survival Depends on Organizing Industry-Wide for Justice and Power." *Labor Research Review* 18: 1–15.

Logan, John. 2008. *US Anti-Union Consultants: A Threat to the Rights of British Workers.* TUC pamphlet series. London: Trades Union Congress.

Kelly, John. 1996. "Union Militancy and Social Partnership." In *The New Workplace and Trade Unionism,* edited by Peter Ackers, Chris Smith, and Paul Smith, 77–109. London: Routledge.

————. 1998. *Rethinking Industrial Relations: Mobilization, Collectivism, and Long Waves.* London: Routledge.

————. 1999. "Social Partnership in Britain: Good for Profits, Bad for Jobs and Unions." *Communist Review* 30 (autumn): 3–10

Kelly, John, and Edmund Heery. 1989. "Full-Time Officers and Trade Union Recruitment." *British Journal of Industrial Relations* 27(2): 196–213.

————. 1994. *Working for the Union: British Trade Union Officers.* Cambridge: Cambridge University Press.

Kersley, Barbara, Carmen Alpin, John Forth, Alex Bryson, Helen Bewley, Gill Dix, and Sarah Oxenbridge. 2006. *Inside the Workplace: Findings from the 2004 Workplace Employment Relations Survey.* London: Routledge

Kimeldorf, Howard. 1999. *Battling For American Labor: Wobblie, Craft Workers and the Making of the Union Movement.* Berkeley: University of California Press.

Kirton, Gill. 2005. "The Influences on Women Joining and Participating in Unions." *Industrial Relations Journal* 36(5): 386–401.

Kirton, Gill, and Gerladine Healy. 1999. "Transforming Union Women: The Role of Female Trade Union Officials." *Industrial Relations Journal* 30(1): 31–45.

————. 2004. "Shaping Union and Gender Identities: A Case Study of Women-Only Trade Union Courses." *British Journal of Industrial Relations* 42(2): 303–323.

Kumar, Pradeep, and Christopher R. Schenk. 2006. "Union Renewal and Organizational Change: A Review of the Literature." In *Paths to Union Renewal: Canadian Experiences,* edited by Pradeep Kumar and Christopher Schenk, 29–60. Toronto: Broadway Press.

Lee, Gloria. 1984. *Trade Unionism and Race: A Report to the West Midlands Regional Council of the Trades Union Congress.* Birmingham, UK: University of Aston Management Centre.

Lerner, Stephen. 2003. "An Immodest Proposal." *New Labor Forum: A Journal of Ideas, Analysis, and Debate* 12: 7–30.

Machin, Stephen. 2000. "Union Decline in Britain." *British Journal of Industrial Relations* 38(4): 631–645.

————. 2001. "The Labour Market Consequences of Technological and Structural Change." *Oxford Bulletin of Economics and Statistics* 63(5): 753–766.

Markowitz, Linda. 2000. *Worker Activism after Successful Union Organizing.* New York: ME Sharpe.

Martínez Lucio, Miguel, and Rob Perrett. 2009. "Meanings and Dilemmas in Community Unionism: Trade Union Community Initiatives and Black and Minority Ethnic Groups in the UK." *Work, Employment, and Society* 23(4): 693–710.

Martínez Lucio, Miguel, Rob Perrett, Jo McBride, and Steve Craig. 2007. *Migrant Workers in the Labour Market: The Role of Unions in the Recognition of Skills and Qualifications.* Unionlearn, Research paper 7. London: TUC.

Martínez Lucio, Miguel, and Mark Stuart. 2009. "Organising and Union Modernisation: Narratives of Renewal in Britain." In *Union Revitalisation in Advanced Economies,* edited by Gregor Gall, 17–37. London: Palgrave Macmillan.

Mason, Bob, and Peter Bain. 1991. "Trade Union Recruitment Strategies: Facing the 1990s." *Industrial Relations Journal* 22(1): 36–45.

McBride, Anne. 2001. *Gender Democracy and Trade Unions.* Aldershot: Ashgate.

McBride, Jo, and Ian Greenwood. 2009. *The Complexity of Community Unionism: A Comparative Analysis of Concepts and Contexts.* Basingstoke: Palgrave Macmillan.

McMullen, John. 2006. "An Analysis of the Transfer of Undertakings (Protection of Employment) Regulations 2006." *Industrial Law Journal* 35(2): 113–139.

Meyerson, Debra. 2003. *Tempered Radicals: How Everyday Leaders Inspire Change at Work.* Boston: Harvard Business School Press.

Michels, Robert. 1915. *Political Parties.* 2nd ed. New York: Free Press.

Milkman, Ruth, and Kim Voss. 2004a. *Rebuilding Labor: Organizing and Organizers in the New Union Movement.* Ithaca: Cornell University Press.

——. 2004b. "Introduction." In *Rebuilding Labor: Organizing and Organizers in the New Union Movement,* edited by Ruth Milkman and Kim Voss, 1–16. Ithaca: Cornell University Press.

Mintzberg, Henry. 1998. "Covert Leadership: Notes on Managing Professionals." *Harvard Business Review?? 76(6) 140–148.*

Moore, Sian. 2004. "Union Mobilization and Employer Counter-Mobilization in the Statutory Recognition Process." In *Union Organization and Activity,* edited by John Kelly and Paul Willman, 7–32. London: Routledge.

Moore, Sian, and Helen Bewley. 2004. *The Content of New Voluntary Trade Union Recognition Agreements 1998–2002: Report of Preliminary Findings.* Employment Relations Research Series No 26. London: UK Department of Trade and Industry.

Mort, Jo-Ann. 1998. *Not Your Father's Union Movement: Inside the AFL-CIO.* New York: Verso.

Nissen, Bruce, and Seth Rosen. 1999. "Community-Based Organizing: Transforming Union Organizing from the Bottom Up." In *Which Direction for Organized Labor? Essays on Organizing, Outreach, and Internal Transformations,* edited by Bruce Nissen, 59–74. Detroit: Wayne State University Press.

Office for National Statistics. Social and Vital Statistics Division and Northern Ireland Statistics and Research Agency. Central Survey Unit, Labour Force Survey 2010. Colchester, Essex: UK Data Archive

Oxenbridge, Sarah, William Brown, Simon Deakin, and Cliff Pratten. 2003. "Initial Responses to the Statutory Recognition Provisions of the Employment Relations Act 1999." *British Journal of Industrial Relations* 41(2): 315–334.

Parker, Jane, and Julie Douglas. 2010. "The Role of Women's Groups in New Zealand, UK, and Canadian Trade Unions in Addressing Intersectional Interests." *International Journal of Comparative Industrial Relations and Labour Law* 26(3): 295–319.

Perrett, Rob, and Miguel Martínez Lucio. 2009. "Trade Unions and Relations with Black and Minority-Ethnic Community Groups in the United Kingdom: The Development of New Alliances?" *Journal of Ethnic and Migration Studies* 35(8): 1295–1314.

Phizacklea, Annie, and Robert Miles. 1987. "The British Trade Union Movement and Racism." In *The Manufacture of Disadvantage: Stigma and Social Closure,* edited by Gloria Lee and Ray Loveridge, 112–125. Milton Keynes: Open University Press.

Portes, Jonathan, and Simon French. 2005. *The Impact of Free Movement of Workers from Central and Eastern Europe on the UK Labour Market: Early Evidence.* Department for Work and Pensions: Working Paper Number 18. London: DWP.

Rachleff, Peter. 1999. "Learning from the Past to Build the Future." In *The Transformation of US Unions: Voices, Visions, and Strategies from the Grassroots,* edited by Ray M. Tillman and Michael S. Cummings, 87–95. Boulder, CO: Lynne Rienner.

Radin, Beryl. 1966. "Coloured Workers and British Trade Unions." *Race* 8: 2.

Reed, Thomas F. 1990. "Profiles of Union Organizers from Manufacturing and Service Unions." *Journal of Labor Research* 11(1): 73–80.

Rooks, Daisy. 2003. "The Cowboy Mentality: Organizers and Occupational Commitment in the New Labor Movement." *Labor Studies Journal* 28: 33–62.

———. 2004. "Sticking It Out Or Packing It In? Organizer Retention in the New Labor Movement." In *Rebuilding Labor: Organizers and Organizers in the New Union Movement,* edited by Ruth Milkman and Kim Voss, 195–224. Ithaca: Cornell University Press.

Schneider, Benjamin. 1980. "The Service Organization: Climate is Crucial." *Organizational Dynamics* 9(2): 52–65.

Sciacchitano, Katherine. 2000. "Unions, Organizing and Democracy." *Dissent* (spring): 75–81.

Sherman, Ruth, and Kim Voss. 2000. "Organize or Die: Labor's New Tactics and Immigrant Workers." In *Organizing Immigrants: The Challenge for Unions in Contemporary California,* edited by Ruth Milkman, 81–108. Ithaca: Cornell University Press.

Simms, Melanie. 2005. "Organising Service Workers: Evidence from Five Trade Union Campaigns." Ph.D. diss., University of Wales, Cardiff.

———. 2006. "The Transition from Organising to Recognition: A Case Study." In *Union Recognition: Organising and Bargaining Outcomes,* edited by Gregor Gall, 167–180. London: Routledge.

———. 2007a. "Managed Activism: Two Union Organizing Campaigns in the Not-for-Profit Sector." *Industrial Relations Journal* 38(2): 119–135.

———. 2007b. "Interest Formation in Greenfield Organising Campaigns." *Industrial Relations Journal* 38(5): 434–454.

Simms, Melanie, and Andy Charlwood. 2010. "Trade Unions: Power and Influence in a Changed Context." In *Industrial Relations: Theory and Practice,* edited by Trevor Colling and Michael Terry, 125–148. London: Wiley.

Simms, Melanie, and Jane Holgate. 2010a. "Organising for What? Where Is the Debate on the Politics of Organising?" *Work, Employment, and Society* 24(1): 157–168

——. 2010b. "10 years of the TUC Organising Academy." *International Journal of Human Resource Management* 21(3): 355–370.

Smith, Paul, and Gary Morton. 2001. "New Labour's Reform of British Employment Law: The Devil Is Not Only in the Detail but in the Values and Policy Too." *British Journal of Industrial Relations* 39(1): 119–138.

——. 2006 "Nine Years of New Labour: Neoliberalism and Workers' Rights." *British Journal of Industrial Relations* 44(3): 401–420.

Stinson, Jane, and Morna Ballantyne. 2006. "Union Renewal and CUPE." In *Paths to Union Renewal: Canadian Experiences,* edited by Pradeep Kumar and Christopher Schenk, 145–160. Peterborough, ON: Broadview Press.

Tattersall, Amanda. 2006. "Bringing the Community In: Possibilities for Public Sector Union Success through Community Unionism." *International Journal of Human Resource Management* 6(2/3/4): 186–199.

——. 2010. *Power in Coalition: Strategies for Strong Unions and Social Change.* Ithaca: Cornell University Press.

TUC. 2007. *General Council Report.* London: Trades Union Congress.

Turner, Lowell, and Richard W. Hurd. 2001. "Building Social Movement Unionism: The Transformation of the American Labor Movement." In *Rekindling the Movement: Labor's Quest for Relevance in the 21st Century,* edited by Lowell Turner, Harry Katz and Richard W. Hurd, 9–26. Ithaca: Cornell University Press.

Turner, Lowell, Harry Katz, and Richard W. Hurd. 2001. *Rekindling the Movement: Labor's Quest for Relevance in the 21st Century.* Ithaca: Cornell University Press.

Undy, Roger. 2002. "New Labour and New Unionism, 1997–2001: But Is It the Same Old Story?" *Employee Relations* 24(6): 638–655.

Virdee, Satnam, and Keith Grint. 1994. "Black Self-Organisation in Trade Unions." *Sociological Review* 42(2): 203–226.

Voss, Kim, and Ruth Sherman. 2000. "Breaking the Iron Law of Oligarchy: Union Revitalization in the American Labor Movement." *American Journal of Sociology* 106(2): 303–349.

Waddington, Jeremy, and Alan Kerr. 2000. "Towards an Organising Model in Unison?" In *Redefining Public Sector Unionism: Unison and the Future of Trade Unionism,* edited by Michael Terry, 231–262. London: Routledge.

——. 2008. "Unions Fit for Young Workers?" *Industrial Relations Journal* 33(4): 298–315.

Walters, Sally. 2002. "Female Part-Time Workers' Attitudes to Trade Unions in Britain." *British Journal of Industrial Relations* 40(1): 49–68.

Wharton, Carol S. 1994. "Finding Time for the 'Second Shift': The Impact of Flexible Work Schedules on Women's Double Days." *Gender and Society* 8: 189–205.

Wheeler, Hoyt. 2002. *The Future of the American Labor Movement.* Cambridge: Cambridge University Press.

Wills, Jane. 2004. "Campaigning for Low Paid Workers: The East London Communities Organisation (TELCO) Living Wage Campaign." In *The Future of Worker*

Representation, edited by William Brown, Geraldine Healy, Edmund Heery, and Phil Taylor, 264–282. Oxford: Oxford University Press.

———. 2005. "The Geography of Union Organising in Low-Paid Service Industries in the UK: Lessons from the T&G's Campaign to Unionise the Dorchester Hotel, London." *Antipode* 37(1): 139–159.

———. 2008. "Making Class Politics Possible: Organizing Contract Cleaners in London." *International Journal of Urban and Regional Research* 32(2): 305–323.

Wills, Jane, and Melanie Simms. 2004. "Building Reciprocal Community Unionism in the UK." *Capital and Class* 82 (spring): 59–84.

Workers Education Association (WEA). 1980. *A Report of a Conference Held in October 1980. Black Workers and Trade Unions.* London: Workers Educational Association.

Index

About the Authors

Melanie Simms is an associate professor in the Industrial Relations and Organisational Behaviour Department at Warwick Business School, University of Warwick, in the United Kingdom. She has researched and published works on the subject of union organizing since 1998. She also has an interest and background in comparative employment relations.

Jane Holgate is a senior lecturer in work and employment relations at the Centre for Employment Relations, Innovation, and Change at the University of Leeds. Jane's research interests include trade unions and the development of organizing and recruitment strategies, particularly as they relate to underrepresented groups, gender and industrial relations, the labor market position of migrants and black and minority ethnic groups, and new geographies of labor and the politics of intersectionality (particularly age, class, and gender)

Edmund Heery is professor of employment relations at Cardiff Business School, Cardiff University. His research interests include trade unions, union organizing, atypical work, equality bargaining, union-community coalitions, civil society organizations and worker representation, and labor relations theory.